365

Bedtime Devotions
for Pre-Teens

Published by Barbour Publishing, Inc., 1810 Barbour Drive, Uhrichsville, Ohio 44683, www.barbourbooks.com

Our mission is to inspire the world with the life-changing message of the Bible.

ecpa Member of the Evangelical Christian Publishers Association

Printed in China.

001861 0124 HA

365
Bedtime Devotions
for Pre-Teens

BARBOUR **kidz**
A Division of Barbour Publishing

Night 1
EVERYTHING!

In the beginning God made from nothing
the heavens and the earth.

GENESIS 1:1

For nearly as long as humans have existed, men and women have tried to figure out how the universe and its people began. But God's Word, the Bible, holds the answer: *everything* came from God, the Great I AM. It's one of those things that you just accept as real—you need to have faith that God *is* and that everything came from Him.

. . . .

Father, many things about You are bigger than I
can understand. When I don't understand, please
help me to simply trust You and believe. Amen.

Night 2
ALWAYS AND FOREVER

God has shown His love to us by sending
His only Son into the world. God did this
so we might have life through Christ.

1 JOHN 4:9

Many things about God are a mystery. We can't understand the ways He works and thinks. But there is one thing we *can* understand: we can know that God loves us. There is nothing we could ever do to make God *stop* loving us, because we did nothing to make Him start. God has *always* loved us because we are His!

You have always loved me, God, and You will love
me forever. Thank You! Compared to Yours, my love
is small, but I love You with all my heart. Amen.

Night 3
THE IMPOSSIBLE

God is able to do much more than we ask or
think through His power working in us.

EPHESIANS 3:20

God's power is greater than any superpower you could ever
imagine. His power and greatness can't be measured. But
we can see it all around us in His creations and the things
He does. And the good news is that He shares it with us!
His power works in us to help us do things that we think
might be impossible. When we pray and ask for God's help,
He will do more for us than we can imagine.

Lord, You do things that really seem impossible. You
know my hopes and dreams, and I believe that You
can—and will!—help me accomplish them. Amen.

Night 4
INSIDE YOUR HEART

Do you not know that you are a house of God
and that the Holy Spirit lives in you?

1 CORINTHIANS 3:16

God's Spirit lives inside us! He is with us wherever we go. So we need to remember to keep our bodies and minds clean and good—like the inside of a church where people go to worship and pray (see 1 Corinthians 6:19 and 2 Corinthians 6:16–17). God's Spirit is living inside your heart right now, and He is *always* with you.

Heavenly Father, how wonderful it is that You
have chosen to live inside me and with me
forever. Help me always to remember that Your
Holy Spirit lives inside my heart. Amen.

Night 5
RULE FOLLOWERS

"Yet they did not obey or listen, but walked in the way
they wanted to and in the strong-will of their sinful
heart. They only stepped back and did not go on."

JEREMIAH 7:24

Humans have never been perfect. Sadly, we often go about
our lives forgetting God's commands, His rules that help
us lead good and happy lives. God wants from us today
what He wanted from people long ago: He wants humans
to follow His rules. The Bible tells us, "Loving God means
to obey His Word" (1 John 5:3). We show God our love by
doing our best to live according to His rules in the Bible.

Sometimes, Lord, I am focused on the world instead of
on You. I'm sorry. Help me to obey Your rules. Amen.

Night 6
GOD'S GIFTS

May you have loving-favor and peace from God our Father and from the Lord Jesus Christ.

1 CORINTHIANS 1:3

✳

The apostle Paul's letters often began like this: *Paul, to (whomever he was writing). May you have loving-favor and peace from God our Father and from the Lord Jesus Christ.* Along with *loving-favor* and *peace*, Paul sometimes added *loving-kindness* to his greeting. These were favors, or blessings, that Paul wished for God to give his friends. Favor, peace, and kindness are God's gifts that help us through life.

Father God, thank You for blessing me daily, and please also bless my family and friends. Amen.

Night 7
WHEN YOU WORRY

When my worry is great within me,
Your comfort brings joy to my soul.

PSALM 94:19

In Psalm 94:19, the writer is so upset that he has no more words to describe his feelings. Instead, he praises God. . . because even when he is all filled up with worry, God is the one who brings him comfort and peace. What do you do when you are filled with worry? Whatever you do, remember this: God knows. He understands. Trust Him to comfort you and work things out.

Dear God, on those days when I am super-
duper upset, please come to me, comfort me,
and remind me to praise You. Amen.

Night 8
JESUS FOLLOWER

They chose Stephen who was a man full
of faith and full of the Holy Spirit.

ACTS 6:5

✳

Some people hated Stephen for talking about Jesus. But he refused to stop telling people to turn their lives around and follow God. He didn't lose his faith even when men dragged him outside and threw big rocks at him. Watching Stephen that sad day was a man named Saul, another Jesus hater. What Saul didn't know then was that someday he would turn his life toward God and become one of the greatest Jesus followers ever.

Lord, please give me a strong faith like Stephen had. Teach me to be a blessing to others and never to be afraid to tell them about You. Amen.

Night 9
TUMBLING-DOWN WALLS

"The city and all that is in it must be destroyed
because everything in it belongs to the Lord."

JOSHUA 6:17

Jericho was a safe place for God's enemies. . .or so they
thought. In their minds, nothing could knock down the city
walls. But God knew better. God planned for His followers
to knock down the walls and take over the city. He com-
manded them to destroy everything inside except gold, silver,
bronze, and iron. Sometimes God's ways are a mystery to
us. Even when we might not understand, He always wants
us to follow His commands. One thing we know is that God
has His reasons for doing what He does. And everything He
does is always right.

God, sometimes Your ways are mysterious to
me. Still, I believe that Your reasons are right,
and I will keep trusting in You. Amen.

Night 10
WISE CHOICES

If you do not have wisdom, ask God for it.
He is always ready to give it to you and will
never say you are wrong for asking. You must
have faith as you ask Him. You must not doubt.
Anyone who doubts. . .will get nothing from the Lord.

JAMES 1:5–7

James said that if we need wisdom, we should never be afraid to ask God, because God wants us to make good choices. When life gets hard, God wants us to have courage. If we trust God when life is hard, He will help us. Faith is the most important message in this scripture passage from James. A strong faith in God is what helps us grow in wisdom and strength.

Father, when life gets hard, help me to trust You.
Open my eyes, Lord. Teach me. Make me wise. Amen.

Night 11
KEEPING SIN AWAY

"This book of the Law must not leave your mouth.
Think about it day and night, so you may be careful to
do all that is written in it. Then all will go well
with you. You will receive many good things."

JOSHUA 1:8

It's easy for sin—bad thoughts and actions—to creep into our
lives. On our computers, tablets, and smartphones, we can
instantly view whatever we want. This is good when we need
information, but it has a not-so-good side too. Joshua 1:8
tells what you should do to keep sin away. Read the Bible!
Study it. Fill your mind with God's Word, day and night, so
you know how God wants you to live. Then follow God's
commands. If you do that, there won't be room in your
heart and mind for sin to creep in.

Dear Lord, plant Your words inside my mind and
heart, and let the Bible always be my guide. Amen.

Night 12
THE GREATEST LOVE

"For God so loved the world that He gave His only Son. Whoever puts his trust in God's Son will not be lost but will have life that lasts forever."

JOHN 3:16

John 3:16 tells us about God's great love. God sent His Son, Jesus, to earth to take our sin away. Jesus was nailed to a cross and left to die. And when He died, our sin died with Him. Then, Jesus rose from the dead. If we believe that Jesus died to take our sin away, then one day we will wake up in heaven, alive and sin-free. That's how much God loves you. He wants you to live with Him forever in heaven!

God, how can I ever thank You for giving us Jesus? I will do my best to show my love for You in everything I say and do. Amen.

Night 13

WHEN YOU DON'T KNOW WHAT TO DO

Trust in the Lord with all your heart, and do not trust in your own understanding. Agree with Him in all your ways, and He will make your paths straight.

PROVERBS 3:5–6

Solomon was a wise king. He knew that our human problem-solving skills don't always measure up. So, Solomon said something like this: "If you don't know what to do, quit trying to figure it out on your own." Solomon knew that God is the only one who has the answers to our problems. The next time you don't know what to do, ask God. Go someplace quiet and tell Him what's going on. Tell Him what you need. Then trust God to work it out. Listen to your heart and believe that God will give you the answer.

Lord, I sometimes run on ahead of You and make decisions on my own. Help me to remember that, even with small decisions, I need Your help. Amen.

Night 14
KEEP WATCH

That is why we must listen all the more
to the truths we have been told. If we do
not, we may slip away from them.

HEBREWS 2:1

In Bible times, fishing boats held four men, and the boat's small size made it dangerous in bad weather. If fishermen were careless about what was happening around them—not noticing a storm brewing—they could find themselves in trouble fast. Their boat would be carried off by the wind and waves. Hebrews 2:1 warns us that we can be like careless fishermen. If we don't keep our eyes open for sin, then sneaky sin can easily carry us away from God. So, keep your eyes open. Watch out for sin, and don't let it carry you away.

Heavenly Father, I know that sin can find many ways to send me off course. Help me to keep my eyes open and my mind set on You. Amen.

Night 15
WONDERFUL BLESSINGS

Then King David went in and sat before the Lord,
and said, "Who am I, O Lord God, and what is my
family, that You have brought me this far?"

2 SAMUEL 7:18

David was just a simple shepherd boy. But because he trusted God, his heavenly Father blessed him in amazing ways. David could not understand why God had given him so much, but he was grateful. God gives you blessings too. Think about all the wonderful things He does for you. Then be like King David. Pray and thank God every day.

Father, thank You! Your blessings are endless
and more than I deserve. Amen.

Night 16
DO YOUR VERY BEST

Love means that we should live by obeying His Word. From the beginning He has said in His Word that our hearts should be full of love.

2 JOHN 1:6

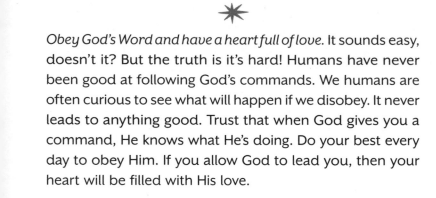

Obey God's Word and have a heart full of love. It sounds easy, doesn't it? But the truth is it's hard! Humans have never been good at following God's commands. We humans are often curious to see what will happen if we disobey. It never leads to anything good. Trust that when God gives you a command, He knows what He's doing. Do your best every day to obey Him. If you allow God to lead you, then your heart will be filled with His love.

God, I want to obey You. Please help me to trust You, especially when I'm curious to see what will happen if I disobey. Amen.

WHAT IS TRUTH?

Pilate said to Jesus, "What is truth?"
After Pilate said this, he went out again to
the Jews. He said, "I do not find Him guilty."

JOHN 18:38

The Roman governor, Pontius Pilate, questioned Jesus and tried to get at the truth. "What is truth?" Pilate asked. But he didn't wait for Jesus' answer. Although in his heart he found Jesus not guilty, Pilate made a sinful decision and allowed the angry crowd to take Jesus to the cross. Always remember: Jesus is all about truth. He is God's Son, the world's Savior. Believe that and listen to His words.

Jesus, You always tell the truth. You are God's
Son and my Savior. Trusting You is the only
way to heaven. Help me always to believe in
You and to listen to Your words. Amen.

Night 18
GOD'S PLAN

It was Hezekiah who stopped the upper
opening of the waters of Gihon, and made
them flow to the west side of the city of David.
And Hezekiah did well in all that he did.

2 CHRONICLES 32:30

✴

Early in Jerusalem's history, a twenty-foot-deep trench covered with rock slabs made a canal that carried water from the spring into a pool inside the walls. This allowed enemy soldiers easy access to the city. A king named Hezekiah solved the problem by covering the outside route to the spring and cutting a tunnel back to the pool. This way, water could be safely gathered and the enemy soldiers kept out. Although Hezekiah's plan was good, it was not as good as God's plan. No one can keep His people from the holy city of Jerusalem.

Wherever the way is blocked, You know a detour.
Whenever there is a problem, You know its solution.
So, lead me, Lord. I want to follow You. Amen.

Night 19
YOUR SAFE PLACE

He who lives in the safe place of the Most High
will be in the shadow of the All-powerful.

PSALM 91:1

✳

The word *shadow* makes us think of a shelter, covering, or protection from heat and storms. Just as a tree's big, leafy branches shield us from the hot sun, God provides us protection wherever we are and whatever problems we face. When we put our trust in Him, we live in the shadow of His protection—a place where nothing can harm us. Whenever you feel afraid, remember that you are not alone. God is with you wherever you go. Talk to Him in prayer and then trust that He will help you.

Most high and almighty God, there is nothing
that can harm me, because You are always
with me. You are my safe place. Amen.

Night 20
FILLED WITH THE WORD

Let the teaching of Christ and His words keep on living in you. These make your lives rich and full of wisdom. Keep on teaching and helping each other. Sing the Songs of David and the church songs and the songs of heaven with hearts full of thanks to God.

COLOSSIANS 3:16

Colossians 3:16 tells us that we become wise when our lives are filled with God's Word. That means we need to study and learn what's in the Bible and keep it in our hearts. The Bible helps us find peace, wisdom, and happiness. Isn't that wonderful? Take time to praise God for giving us His special book, the Bible. Then spread some of God's wisdom around. Share the Word of God with your friends.

Dear Jesus, may my words and my actions
be a reflection of Your Word, the Bible,
and pleasing in Your sight. Amen.

Night 21
A WILLING HEART

While Jesus was in one of the towns, a man came to Him with a bad skin disease over all his body. When he saw Jesus, he got down on his face before Him. He begged Him, saying, "Lord, if You are willing, You can heal me." Jesus put His hand on him and said, "I will, be healed."

LUKE 5:12–13

A sick man asked Jesus if He was willing to heal him. Of course Jesus was willing! Jesus wants us to be willing too, like He was. He wants us to be willing to do His work here on earth. He wants us to try to be more like Him—kind, caring, and willing to help. Ask Jesus to show you what He wants you to do. Then keep your eyes open for ways that you can help others. Don't worry that you aren't old enough, smart enough, or strong enough to do great things. Jesus will give you the power to do His work as long as you are willing.

Jesus, I am willing. Use me. Work through me to accomplish whatever You want. Whether it is something great or something small, I am ready. Amen.

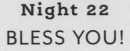

Night 22
BLESS YOU!

"The LORD bless you and keep you."
NUMBERS 6:24 NKJV

✳

"God bless you." Has someone ever said that to you? Maybe you've heard it in Sunday school or church or from your parents. But what do the words *God bless you* mean? To be blessed by God means that He covers you with His goodness and protection; He does good things for you. God loves and protects you. So, be happy and celebrate His blessings. Give praise and thanks to God for all the wonderful ways He blesses you.

• •

Thank You, Lord, for the many blessings You give me each day. Morning and night You bless me, and I am so grateful! Amen.

Night 23
MISSION ACCOMPLISHED

Jesus took the sour wine and said,
"It is finished." He put His head down
and gave up His spirit and died.

JOHN 19:30

✳

God always has a plan, and His plan is always perfect. God had a purpose for Jesus—salvation. Jesus' purpose was to save people from sin. God allowed His own Son to die in our place so someday we could live in heaven. Just before Jesus died on the cross, He said the words "It is finished." He meant that God's plan to save us was done. Mission accomplished! From that day forward, anyone who believed in Jesus and asked for forgiveness of their sins would be welcomed into heaven.

Thank You, Jesus, for completing God's plan of salvation. Thank You for saving me from sin. Amen.

Night 24
JUST AS YOU ARE

"There is not one person who is
right with God. No, not even one!"

ROMANS 3:10

God is the only one who is, always has been, and always will be perfect. No human can ever be as perfect as He is. We all have times when we sin by disobeying God's rules. Because we can't help sinning sometimes, we can't be perfect like God. That's why we need Jesus—to clean away our sin so someday we can live with God forever in heaven. Ask Jesus to be your Savior, and then do your very best to live a good life for Him. That is what God wants from you. Because of Jesus, He loves you and accepts you just the way you are!

God, on days when I feel not good enough for You,
myself, or others, I come to You believing that
You will accept me just as I am. Amen.

Night 25
A FOREVER LIFE

"But God raised Him up. He allowed Him to
be set free from the pain of death. Death
could not hold its power over Him."

ACTS 2:24

Jesus told His followers that three days after He died on the
cross, He—body and all—would come back from the dead.
And that is exactly what happened. Jesus' resurrection—His
body coming to life again—was God's way of showing the
world that Jesus really was who He said He was. . .God's
Son, the Messiah who came to save us from sin. Death had
no power over Jesus, and it has no power over us either. If
we believe in Him, then we will wake up someday to a new,
forever life in heaven.

Lord, I praise You because You are the only one
who brings forever life to all believers. Thanks to You,
I look forward to a new life in heaven someday. Amen.

Night 26
THE RIGHT THING

But when Peter came to Antioch, I had to
stand up against him because he was guilty.

GALATIANS 2:11

Sometimes people make wrong choices because they don't know any better. Sometimes they choose wrong because they want to fit in with their friends. God wants us to be strong and do what we know is right. That's why it's so important to know and follow God's rules. You will learn His rules by reading the Bible. If you know God's rules, then, like Paul did, you might even help someone else if you see that person making a wrong choice. Pray and ask God to teach you and guide you so when you are faced with a decision, you will make the right choice.

God, guide me in Your ways. Help me to learn Your rules so that I will make good choices in my life. Amen.

Night 27
WORKING TOGETHER

Next to them Uzziel the son of Harhaiah,
who worked with gold, did the needed work.
Next to him Hananiah, one of the men who
made perfume, did the needed work. They made
Jerusalem like new as far as the Wide Wall.

NEHEMIAH 3:8

The Bible's Old Testament tells about Nehemiah, a cupbearer
to the king of Persia. When Nehemiah heard that most of
Jerusalem had been destroyed by enemy soldiers, he asked
the king for permission to leave his job to do God's work.
His goal was to rebuild the broken city.

Nehemiah called on all who believed in God to help.
And together, they worked side by side, and *in just fifty-two
days*, they rebuilt Jerusalem and its walls! That's how God
expects us to work today, side by side with other believers.

Heavenly Father, lead me to work together
with others who believe in You. Please guide
us toward You and Your work. Amen.

Night 28
THINK AND PRAY

But Mary hid all these words in her heart.
She thought about them much.

LUKE 2:19

When Jesus was born, angels appeared to shepherds watching over their sheep. The angels told the shepherds that the baby born nearby, in Bethlehem, was God's Son—the one who would save the world from sin. The shepherds went to see the baby, and they told Mary what the angels had said. The Bible does not tell us exactly what Mary thought. It just says that she thought much about the responsibility of raising Jesus. Certainly, she prayed and asked God to guide her. Whenever you face an important responsibility, take time to think and pray first.

Sometimes, Lord, I jump right into something without taking time to think about what You want me to do. Remind me to slow down, maybe even stop, and turn my thoughts toward You. Amen.

Night 29
GOD HELPS YOU BELIEVE

The Lord said to him, "What is that in your hand?"
EXODUS 4:2

Have you ever experienced a miracle? The Bible tells us that Moses did. God surprised Moses by setting a bush on fire and appearing in its flames. He told Moses that He had chosen him to lead the Israelites out of Egypt to God's Promised Land. But Moses wasn't sure he would be a good leader for the people. It took several miracles for Moses to believe that God would help him and be with him. Maybe you are like Moses and you aren't sure that God is with you all the time. If you ask God to help you believe, He certainly will!

Heavenly Father, I do my best to believe You are always with me, but sometimes I need reassurance. Help me, please, to believe. Amen.

Night 30
WORDS TO REMEMBER

Your heart should be holy and set apart for
the Lord God. Always be ready to tell everyone
who asks you why you believe as you do.
Be gentle as you speak and show respect.

1 PETER 3:15

Peter wrote to give Christians advice about how to set a
Christlike example and what to say if anyone asked them
about Jesus. First, he told them to make God more important in their hearts than anything else. Second, Peter told
his friends to be ready to tell nonbelievers that Jesus came
to save them from sin so they might live forever in heaven.
Finally, Peter wrote that they should explain Jesus to nonbelievers with gentleness and respect. Remember Peter's
words, because someday one of your friends might ask you
about Jesus. Will you be ready?

Dear God, please prepare me to explain Jesus to
anyone who asks. Teach me to explain in a way
that honors You with gentleness and respect. Amen.

Night 31
GOOD THINGS

A man's wisdom makes his face shine.
The hard look on his face is changed.

ECCLESIASTES 8:1

✳

Even on bad days, your face can wear a smile. A wise way
to boost your attitude is to think about God's blessings. In
one of his letters, Paul wrote, "Keep your minds thinking
about whatever is true, whatever is respected, whatever is
right, whatever is pure, whatever can be loved, and whatever is well thought of. If there is anything good and worth
giving thanks for, think about these things" (Philippians 4:8).

Father, put a smile on my face tomorrow
morning. Bless me with a good attitude
that I can share with others. Amen.

Night 32
LISTENING TO JESUS

Jesus said to them, "You are wrong
because you do not know the Holy
Writings or the power of God."

MATTHEW 22:29

The Sadducees, a rich and powerful religious group in Jesus' time, tried to trap Him into saying that He was not the Son of God. They asked Him question after question, trying to make Him contradict Himself. Jesus knew what they were up to. He basically told them that they didn't know what they were talking about, because they didn't know God or what's in the Bible. If they did, they would *know* that He was the Son of God. Imagine being alive during the time Jesus was teaching and being able to hear the voice of the Son of God as He spoke!

God, as I read Your Word, open my eyes to Your truth.
Teach me Your ways so that I may apply them to
my life and walk in the footsteps of Jesus. Amen.

Night 33
LOVING OTHERS WELL

Jesus said to him, " 'You must love the Lord
your God with all your heart and with all
your soul and with all your mind.' "

MATTHEW 22:37

Everything Jesus ever taught and lived revolved around love.
Everything Jesus did, He did with love. Even when He was
angry with people, it was because He knew their actions
were going opposite of God's will. There was never a time
when Jesus spoke to another person, went anywhere, or
did anything without being filled with love for people. This
is how we should live too. Our Lord is the God of love, and
there is nothing more important. We should be like Jesus and
focus on what is right with the world and with other people.

I sometimes find it hard to focus on the goodness
in people. Change me, Lord. Lead me to love
others just as You love them. Amen.

Night 34
PROMISE OF HEAVEN

I say to myself, "The LORD is my portion;
therefore I will wait for him."

LAMENTATIONS 3:24 NIV

The word *portion* means a part of something that is yours. The writer of today's verse says that the Lord is his potion. He meant that everything God is and does belongs to him. This applies to all of us. God promises us a portion of something else. . .heaven! He promises that if we believe in Jesus, we already have a home waiting for us there when we die. You will likely have to wait a long time before you get to meet God in heaven face-to-face. But you can be sure that when you get there, a beautiful home will be waiting for you.

What an amazing promise You have made to me,
Father, that one day I will be with You in heaven.
My hope is in You as I wait for that day. Amen.

Night 35
THE SECRET TO A GREAT MORNING

Let me hear Your loving-kindness
in the morning, for I trust in You.

PSALM 143:8

King David, the man who wrote Psalm 143, had learned the secret to getting each morning off to a good start. He chose to begin every day thinking about God's love. It didn't matter to David if the sun was shining or if he'd had a good night's sleep. It didn't matter if David was worried about a problem. He made a choice to trust God first thing every morning, no matter what. Thinking about God's love throughout the day reminded David that the Lord was with him, not only in the morning, but also all day long and through the night.

God, I wake up in the morning, and You are there. You are with me all day long and throughout the night. Thank You, heavenly Father, for Your never-ending love. Amen.

Night 36
GOD'S BOOK

"Everyone who has power and wins will wear
white clothes. I will not take his name from
the book of life. I will speak of his name
before My Father and His angels."

REVELATION 3:5

*

This Bible verse is about people who have believed in and
accepted Jesus as their Savior. When a believer dies and
goes to heaven, that person will wear spotless white clothes.
Jesus will speak the person's name to God and His angels.
Can you imagine what a great introduction that would be?
A believer's name will never be erased from God's book. It
will stay there forever.

• •

Thank You, dear God, for caring so much about me that
You've written my name in Your heavenly book. Amen.

Night 37
EVERYWHERE,
ALL THE TIME!

"But is it true that God will live on the earth?
See, heaven and the highest heaven are
not big enough to hold You. How much
less this house which I have built!"

1 KINGS 8:27

When his temple was finished, Solomon felt God's presence there, but he also realized something else: God is not in just one place. *He is everywhere all at the same time!* God Himself says, "Am I not everywhere in all the heavens and earth?" (Jeremiah 23:24 NLT). He sees and cares for each of us. God knows where we are, both day and night, and guides us through good and bad times. Isn't that wonderful?

You know exactly where I am, God. I call and You
hear me. Thank You, Lord! I love You! Amen.

Night 38
GIVE IT TO JESUS

"Come to Me, all of you who work and have heavy loads. I will give you rest. Follow My teachings and learn from Me. I am gentle and do not have pride. You will have rest for your souls. For My way of carrying a load is easy and My load is not heavy."

MATTHEW 11:28–30

✳

Here in Matthew, Jesus is speaking to everyone who feels stressed out. "Come to Me," He says. "I will give you rest." Jesus meant that we should trust Him with everything in life. When we have a problem that weighs us down, we can bring it to Jesus in our prayers. We can give to Him whatever stresses us out and have faith that He will handle it for us. It is His promise to us. And Jesus always keeps His promises. Has something been bothering you lately? Give it to Jesus, and then relax. You can trust Him to work it out.

• •

Jesus, I'm glad that You want to take on
my troubles. I give them to You right now,
and I trust You to give me rest. Amen.

Night 39
GOD FORGIVES

If we tell Him our sins, He is faithful and we
can depend on Him to forgive us of our sins.
He will make our lives clean from all sin.

1 JOHN 1:9

✳

Maybe you feel awful after you've done something wrong.
You hear a little voice in your heart that keeps reminding
you of what you did. Would you like that voice to go away?
Here's how: 1 John 1:9 teaches us that if we pray to God and
tell Him we are sorry for our sins, He will forgive us. God
cleans away our sin. We all sin, every one of us! God knows
that, and He wants to fix it. You can trust Him to forgive you
and heal your guilty feelings.

God, sometimes I feel so ashamed of my
sins that I avoid confessing them to You. Help
me to remember that You will forgive me,
if I just come to You and ask. Amen.

Night 40
CITIZENS OF HEAVEN

But we are citizens of heaven. Christ, the One Who
saves from the punishment of sin, will be coming down
from heaven again. We are waiting for Him to return.

PHILIPPIANS 3:20

✳

If you have accepted Jesus as your Savior, you already have a
home waiting for you in heaven. You don't have to do anything
else to become a citizen there. Paul tells us in Philippians
3:20 that we already are citizens of heaven, even while we
live here on earth. As heaven's citizens, we will enjoy all the
rights and privileges of our heavenly Father. Meanwhile, God
wants us to act like heavenly citizens while we live here on
earth. This means putting Him first in our thoughts and acting
in ways that please Him.

Heavenly Father, thank You for Your gift
of salvation. As a Christian, I know that my
forever home is there with You in heaven.
I cannot imagine how wonderful it is! Amen.

A GIFT FOR LOYAL HEARTS

"For the eyes of the Lord move over all the earth so that He may give strength to those whose whole heart is given to Him."

2 CHRONICLES 16:9

God wants to find hearts committed to knowing Him and learning His ways. God is looking for people who want to talk and listen to Him and who are willing to serve and please Him. God gives loyal hearts a gift—His strength. God looks all over the earth for those who will love Him. He searches our hearts and knows if we welcome Him there. When we open our hearts to receive Him, He will find us.

. . . .

Find me, Lord. Pull me close to You.
Open my heart so that I may fully receive
all You want to pour into it. Amen.

Night 42
WHAT LIFE'S ALL ABOUT

When Jesus heard that John had been killed,
He went from there by boat to a desert.
He wanted to be alone. When the people knew it,
they followed after Him by land from the cities.

MATTHEW 14:13

✳

When His cousin died, Jesus wanted to be left alone for a while. He went out onto the sea in a boat in search of peace. When Jesus came back to the shore and saw the people, "He had loving-pity for them and healed those who were sick" (Matthew 14:14). Then, Jesus fed five thousand people with five loaves of bread and two fish. Feeling sorry for ourselves shouldn't last forever. Life isn't about us; it's about the wonderful things we can do for God when we put our own sadness behind us and turn our thoughts toward others.

Dear God, when I feel sorry for myself, remind
me to think about what others need. Amen.

Night 43
FROM DEATH TO LIFE!

The Holy Spirit proved by a powerful act
that Jesus our Lord is the Son of God
because He was raised from the dead.

ROMANS 1:4

Jesus told the Jewish people, "I am the Son of God." He also told them that if they didn't believe, they *should* because of the miracles He did (John 10:36–38). Still, some people did not believe. Final proof came when God's Holy Spirit raised Jesus back to life after He was in the grave for three days. That same powerful Spirit that raised Jesus from the dead lives inside our hearts. It reminds us that Jesus is God's Son, and if we believe, we will live with Him forever in heaven.

Jesus, I believe You are the Son of God. I know that
God's powerful Holy Spirit raised You from death,
and someday He will do the same for me. Amen.

Night 44
SEEING LIKE JESUS

You do well when you obey the Holy Writings which say,
"You must love your neighbor as you love yourself."

JAMES 2:8

✳

Sometimes you think about His commandments and what
Jesus taught, and you wonder if you are living well enough
for God to want you in heaven someday. James 2:8 shows
us that we are living as we should if we obey God's law to
love one another. This isn't always easy. Some people are,
well—just difficult to love! Sometimes it's so hard to see
others as Jesus does. But, if we try to see people through
the eyes of Jesus, that's good enough for God. When we
do our best, then in God's eyes we are doing well.

Give me Your eyes, Lord. Allow me to see others
as You see them. Then, with Your help, I can
love those who seem unlovable. Amen.

Night 45
A CHILD OF GOD

The Lord God planted a garden to the east in Eden.
He put the man there whom He had made.

GENESIS 2:8

✳

We humans have given in to sin from the start, and we often don't think we deserve God's forgiveness and love. We might think that heaven is for perfect people—not weak, scared people who mess up, like us. And when we think like that, we break God's heart. He isn't waiting for us to prove ourselves worthy of His love. He made us, He loves us, and He wants us to be with Him forever. Remember this: God loves you just as you are, sin and all. He made you. You are His child.

• •

Thank You for loving me,
God, just the way I am. Amen.

Night 46
GOD IS IN CHARGE

Then the demons brought the kings together in the place called Armageddon in the Hebrew language.

REVELATION 16:16

✳

The Bible says that the last war on earth will be fought in Armageddon. But Christians don't have to be afraid, because God is in charge. The Bible tells us that God wins this last earthly battle. Afterward, He will create a new and perfect earth. It will be as perfect as the garden of Eden was *before* Adam and Eve sinned. Then, everyone whose name is written in God's heavenly book will live on His perfect earth forever. God wants you to follow Jesus. You belong to Him, and He will take care of you today and every day.

• •

Father, I will live happily and not be afraid.
I know that You are in charge and that
You will take care of me. Amen.

Night 47
COURAGEOUS TRUST

I am asking you for my son, Onesimus.
He has become my son in the Christian
life while I have been here in prison.

PHILEMON 1:10

While in Rome, Onesimus—a runaway slave—became a
follower of Jesus. He realized he needed to do the right
thing: return to his owner and give back what he had stolen.
However, doing so could mean his death. Determined to
do the right thing whatever the cost, Onesimus made plans
to return. Onesimus displayed great courage and trust in
Jesus by returning to Philemon. How courageous are you
in your trust? Are you willing to trust Jesus to help you do
what is right?

God, please strengthen my trust in Jesus.
Take away anything that prevents me
from doing what's right. Amen.

Night 48
FRIENDS WHO KNOW JESUS

When Joshua was by Jericho, he looked up and
saw a man standing near him with his sword
in his hand. Joshua went to him and said,
"Are you for us or for those who hate us?"

JOSHUA 5:13

God wants us to be careful about the people we choose
to hang out with. Are they for God or against Him? Those
who are for God lead us closer to Him. They always do their
best to live in ways that please Him. Those who are against
God don't know Him. They live carefree, sinful lives and try
to convince others to do things that they know are wrong.
Be careful when choosing your friends. Be close with those
who love God. And pray that the others change their lives
and learn to honor Him.

Father, help me to choose my friends wisely and to
remember to pray for those who don't know You. Amen.

Night 49
WALKING ON WATER

Jesus said, "Come!" Peter got out of the
boat and walked on the water to Jesus.

MATTHEW 14:29

The Bible describes times when Jesus, the perfect Son of
God, broke the rules of physics by walking on the waves.
But there was someone far from perfect who also walked
on water: Jesus' disciple Peter. Humans today don't walk on
water; but ordinary people who follow God's commands
have successfully accomplished difficult, even impossible,
tasks. So, don't give up when things seem hard. That's the
perfect time to rely on God's strength.

You are my strength, Lord. Whenever I feel like
giving up, I will turn to You for help. Amen.

Night 50
MORE LIKE JESUS

Be holy in every part of your life. Be like the
Holy One Who chose you. The Holy Writings
say, "You must be holy, for I am holy."

1 PETER 1:15–16

✴

Our heavenly Father wants us to work to be like Jesus. He had a human body like ours, one that could hurt, bleed, and die; but in every other way, Jesus was perfectly perfect. He is our example of how to live. The more we become like Him, the more pleasing our lives are to God. You should keep doing your best to be holy in all that you do. Be kind, caring, and giving. Keep your mind focused on God. You won't be perfect on earth, no matter how hard you try. But when you get to heaven someday, you will be perfectly holy with God.

I give myself to You, Father, a work in progress.
Come into my heart. Shape me and direct
me so that I might please You. Amen.

Night 51
GOD WORKS THROUGH YOU!

Peter said, "I have no money, but what I
have I will give you! In the name of Jesus
Christ of Nazareth, get up and walk!"

ACTS 3:6

✳

A man who couldn't walk sat outside the temple and
begged. Peter and John had no money to give him. "Peter
said, 'I have no money, but what I have I will give you! In
the name of Jesus Christ of Nazareth, get up and walk!' . . .
At once his feet and the bones in his legs became strong.
He jumped up. . .and walked" (Acts 3:6–8)! God had done
a miraculous thing through Peter. God will work through
you too. You probably won't heal someone, but you can
be generous with others through your kindness and caring
and by sharing your talents.

· ·

God, please work through me. Guide me to use
what You have given me to help others. Amen.

Night 52
CLOSER TO GOD

Lappidoth's wife Deborah, a woman who spoke
for God, was judging Israel at that time.

JUDGES 4:4

✳

Deborah was a prophet, a judge, and a military leader. A
prophet is someone called by God to speak on His behalf.
Deborah inspired people to turn their hearts toward God.
Deborah is a role model for *everyone* today. We may not
see ourselves as leaders, but we all can draw others closer
to God. Think about ways you can lead others to Him. Keep
your eyes open for opportunities. Every day, your simple
acts of kindness can draw others closer to God.

Heavenly Father, open my eyes and my heart!
Lead me to share You with others. Amen.

Night 53
SHARING JESUS

"This Good News about the holy nation of God
must be preached over all the earth. It must be
told to all nations and then the end will come."

MATTHEW 24:14

You might think that in this modern age the gospel has
already been preached in all nations through missionaries,
radios, television, the internet. . .but there are groups of
people in far-off parts of the world who have not heard of
Jesus yet. That's why it's important for you to pray and do
your part to see that these people hear about Him. There is
still work to be done before Jesus returns. Everyone needs to
know about Him, in every country to the ends of the earth!

Lord, there are still people who haven't
heard about You. Remind me to pray
for those who need to hear. Amen.

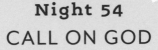

Night 54
CALL ON GOD

Your ears will hear a word behind you,
saying, "This is the way, walk in it,"
whenever you turn to the right or to the left.

ISAIAH 30:21

Everyone faces big decisions sometimes, and today's Bible verse offers encouragement and hope to those who call on God. When we turn to Him in trust and use His navigational system, the Bible, we can be sure that His map for our lives is perfect. Unlike any earthly directions, God will never lead us down dead-end roads or send us onto nonexistent streets. Instead, He promises to hear us when we cry for help (see Isaiah 30:19). And from that moment on, He gives us directions that we can trust 100 percent.

I'm thankful, Father, for Your God Positioning System.
Each morning, remind me to turn it on so that Your
voice can direct me in the way I should go. Amen.

Night 55
LOVE AND KINDNESS

If a person says, "I love God," but hates his brother, he
is a liar. If a person does not love his brother whom he
has seen, how can he love God Whom he has not seen?

1 JOHN 4:20

Do your best to be kind to those who are unkind to you. It's
difficult, and God does not want you to get hurt or in trouble, but do your best to love them like Jesus would. Maybe
there are those who have hurt you, people you trusted once
and find hard to forgive. God wants you to forgive them
and replace the hurt with love. It's a big assignment and
one that might not always work, but you will be nearer to
God for having tried!

God, sometimes it's hard acting in a Christlike
way, especially toward those who are not my
friends. Help me, please, to love everyone,
not just those who love me back. Amen.

Night 56
BLESSING ENEMIES

If the one who hates you is hungry, feed him.
If he is thirsty, give him water. If you do that,
you will be making him more ashamed of
himself, and the Lord will reward you.

PROVERBS 25:21–22

God says to find ways to be kind to your enemy. It may be hard to gather up the courage to show kindness to someone who is not your friend, but God will give you His strength. And God also hints in this verse that your kindness might make that person feel ashamed of the way you were treated. It might help that person turn to God. Whatever happens as a result of your goodness, God promises to reward you for trying.

Dear Lord, help me to be forgiving toward my enemies. Even if they hate me, teach me to bless them by showing them love. Amen.

Night 57
HONORING GOD

In those days King Ahasuerus sat on the. . .throne in the city of Susa. In the third year of his rule, he gave a special supper for all his princes and leaders. . . . There was much wine, because the king was very able and willing to give it. . . . The king had told all the workmen of his house that they should give each person what he wanted.

ESTHER 1:2–3, 7–8

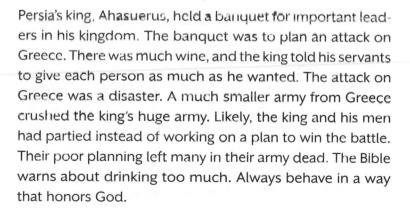

Persia's king, Ahasuerus, held a banquet for important leaders in his kingdom. The banquet was to plan an attack on Greece. There was much wine, and the king told his servants to give each person as much as he wanted. The attack on Greece was a disaster. A much smaller army from Greece crushed the king's huge army. Likely, the king and his men had partied instead of working on a plan to win the battle. Their poor planning left many in their army dead. The Bible warns about drinking too much. Always behave in a way that honors God.

Lord, as I get older, please keep me away from alcohol and drugs. I want to live to please You. Amen.

THE KEY TO HEAVEN

Jesus looked at them and said, "This cannot be done by men. But with God all things can be done."

MATTHEW 19:26

✳

A rich young ruler asked Jesus what he needed to do to get to heaven. Jesus told him to sell his possessions and give to the poor. The rich man went home feeling sad. Jesus said no one can be saved by their own efforts! The rich young ruler had tried everything humanly possible, and still he failed. His best efforts could never measure up to God's requirements. Only accepting God's grace—His forgiveness and favor, even when we don't deserve it—will admit us to heaven. Realizing we can do *nothing* is the key to gaining *everything*—God's gift of heaven!

Dear Father, thank You for Your grace—
Your loving-kindness that I don't deserve.
There is nothing I have done to earn it.
Grace is Your gift to me. Amen.

Night 59
PLANNING AHEAD

Go to the ant, O lazy person. Watch and
think about her ways, and be wise.

PROVERBS 6:6

Each species of ants—over ten thousand—forms colonies that
consist of one or more queens, a few males, and numerous
female worker ants. Proverbs 6:6 compares these hardwork-
ing ants with lazy people. But sometimes people aren't lazy
at all. Some just feel overwhelmed by the size of a task. If
that describes you, then break a chore into small parts and
celebrate completing each one. Become wise by planning
ahead. Study the ants and learn from them.

When a task seems so big and impossible,
remind me, Lord, that You will help me to
accomplish it, one small step at a time. Amen.

Night 60
THE STORY OF JESUS

*There are many other things which Jesus
did also. If they were all written down,
I do not think the world itself could hold
the books that would be written.*

JOHN 21:25

Jesus' disciple John said that to write a complete biography
of Jesus' life would require more books than the world has
room for! So, when John chose which details of Jesus' life
to include in his Gospel—he did it with great care. All the
Gospel writers did. They each had a particular purpose in
writing their accounts of Jesus' life. Jesus' story continues to
be written—in us. The way we live our lives can lead others
to faith in Him.

Jesus, the Gospels make me want to know more
about You. Teach me to become more like You
and to grow nearer to You as I learn. Amen.

Night 61
FOR THE BEST

Never stop praying.

1 THESSALONIANS 5:17

When we pray and tell God what is in our hearts, He always finds a way to bless us and make everything work out for the best. God is so much smarter than we could ever hope to be. He knows what is best for us and provides it each time. All we have to do is share our concerns with Him and wait for what He will provide. God never promised an easy life to Christians. If we will allow Him, though, God will be there with us every step of the way, every day of our lives.

Father, when I pray, remind me that prayer is not only about talking to You but also about listening to You. Open my heart to Your words. Amen.

Night 62
CARRYING GOD'S WORDS

"Keep these words of mine in your heart and in your soul. Tie them as something special to see upon your hand and on your forehead between your eyes. Teach them to your children. Talk about them when you sit in your house and when you walk on the road and when you lie down and when you get up. Write them beside the door of your house and on your gates."

DEUTERONOMY 11:18–20

How do we Christians carry God's Word with us all the time? By keeping important Bible verses in our hearts and minds. Memorizing Bible verses reminds us that God is always with us. Give it a try!

What an awesome gift You have given me, God—the Bible! I will remember Your words and carry them with me wherever I go. Amen.

Night 63
CALMING THE STORM

He said to them, "Where is your faith?" The
followers were surprised and afraid. They said to
each other, "What kind of a man is He? He speaks
to the wind and the waves and they obey Him."

LUKE 8:25

It was calm on the lake that day when the disciples and
Jesus set out in their boat to sail to the other side. During the
gentle boat ride, Jesus fell asleep. Then it happened—a storm.
The disciples woke Jesus and begged Him to do something
because they were going to drown. Jesus got up and spoke
to the wind and the waves. The storm stopped. Jesus used
the terrifying boat ride not only to display His power over
all creation but to provide an opportunity for the disciples
to look at the depth of their faith. Do you believe that Jesus
can do anything?

Jesus, increase my faith. Teach me to trust even more
in Your power and Your ability to calm the storms
that come into my life. I love You, Lord Jesus. Amen.

THE RIGHT ANSWER

Do not answer a fool by his foolish ways, or you will be like him. Answer a fool in the way he has earned by his foolish acts, so he will not be wise in his own eyes.

PROVERBS 26:4–5

✳

These verses from Proverbs seem to give two opposite pieces of advice. The author, King Solomon, did this on purpose to make it clear that we are to respond differently in different circumstances. Maybe you know someone who always thinks he is right. Maybe you know what that person says is foolish and wrong. What you should say to that person depends on the situation. God may lead you to give him a serious answer or a humorous, foolish answer (to show him how foolishly he's talking). Or sometimes, God might lead you to say nothing at all.

Dear God, when I don't know how to respond to a foolish opinion, show me. Give me the right answer or lead me to be still. Amen.

Night 65
JESUS UNDERSTANDS

Then Jesus cried.

JOHN 11:35

✳

As God's Son on earth, Jesus felt things as we humans do. He laughed and He cried. Jesus cried over the death of His friend Lazarus. Jesus' great miracle was raising Lazarus from the dead. This proved His power as God's Son—but before that, just like humans, Jesus cried over the loss of a friend. Jesus still feels our pain when we cry. And we can count on Him to comfort us. The next time you feel sad, remember that Jesus is right there with you, and He understands.

Jesus, when things in life make me cry, remind me that You care and understand. Hug me, Lord. Hold me in Your arms and comfort me. Amen.

GOD IS THE BEST GUIDE

"Then you will know which way to go,
since you have never been this way before.
But keep a distance of about two thousand
cubits between you and the ark; do not go near it."

JOSHUA 3:4 NIV

Joshua led the Israelites across the Jordan River into a new land. The plan was for them to follow the ark (a chest that contained the stones onto which God wrote the Ten Commandments), which the priests would carry. When they saw the direction the ark was going, they would know which way to go. The Israelites could only safely travel into the unknown by believing that God was leading them. Many times in your life, you are going to find yourself heading in a direction you are not familiar with. When God brings you to that unknown territory, you can be sure He'll guide you through it.

Sometimes You lead me into unfamiliar places,
Father, but You always bring me through them.
You know the way. Thank You, God! Amen.

Night 67
JESUS IS LOVE

"But I tell you, do not fight with the man who wants to fight. Whoever hits you on the right side of the face, turn so he can hit the other side also."

MATTHEW 5:39

Jesus is all about love. He said we should love God (Matthew 22:36–37), love our neighbors (Matthew 22:39), and love our enemies (Matthew 5:44)! It sounds great, but loving our enemies can be difficult. God knows we live in a world where walking away is often judged as cowardly. That's why He sent Jesus to be our example of love. Think about it: when Jesus was nailed to the cross by an angry mob, He prayed, "Father, forgive them" (Luke 23:34). Do your very best to avoid any kind of fight. Battle against anger with love and ask God to help you love your enemies.

Heavenly Father, when someone does wrong to me, please quiet my anger and soothe my hurt. Help me to love my enemies with Your kind of love. Amen.

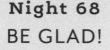

Night 68
BE GLAD!

Be glad you can do the things you should be doing.
Do all things without arguing and talking about
how you wish you did not have to do them.

PHILIPPIANS 2:14

If anyone had a right to complain, it was Jesus' friend Paul.
He had a tough life. Paul had suffered through shipwrecks,
had been made fun of, beaten, and put into prison for doing
nothing wrong. Still, he wrote the words of Philippians 2:14:
"Be glad." Complaining is something all humans do. But God
wants us to be like Paul, turn that around, and have a positive attitude. Think every day about how God has blessed
you. Do willingly what you don't want to do. Be happy and
replace your grumbles with sunshine.

Lord, I argue and complain, and often I
am not even aware of my bad attitude.
Remind me to look on the bright side and
to share a little sunshine with others. Amen.

Night 69
FOCUS ON GOD

While Paul was waiting for Silas and Timothy
in Athens, his spirit was troubled as he saw
the whole city worshiping false gods.

ACTS 17:16

When God gave the Ten Commandments to Moses, the very
first one was "Have no gods other than Me" (Exodus 20:3).
The people in Moses' time did not obey these commands,
and humans don't obey them still. Our false gods today
are usually everyday things that we make more important
than God. For some people, money is the most important
thing. Others might worship a person or even an idea. The
best way to make God your only God is to keep your mind
on Him all the time. Don't allow anything to become more
important than Him.

Dear God, I want You to be my one and only God.
Please help me to stay focused on You. Amen.

Night 70
PERFECT HEART-VISION

Turn my eyes away from things that have no worth,
and give me new life because of Your ways.

PSALM 119:37

✳

Some things in life take our eyes off Jesus and pull us further away from Him—things that distract us, like television shows and video games. Other things, like worrying about what might happen tomorrow or next week, keep us from seeing what God is doing for us right now. Perfect heart-vision comes when we remember to keep God's Word in our hearts and focus our thoughts always on Him. Are there things in your life that are keeping you from having perfect vision of the heart? Think about it. What changes can you make to focus your heart on Jesus?

Jesus, there are so many distractions in life, things
that get in my way. Help me to make them less
important and to keep my focus on You. Amen.

NOTICE GOD'S BLESSINGS

Give me your heart, my son.
Let your eyes find joy in my ways.

PROVERBS 23:26

We find joy by knowing that God is in control of our lives, and He wants only what is best for us. Sometimes God allows us to experience difficult things because those things build up our faith in Him. At other times, God will bless us with something to be joyful about when we feel discouraged, frustrated, or sad. Proverbs 23:26 reminds us that we should keep our eyes open for God's blessings and not allow circumstances to keep us from noticing them. Remember *always* that God is in your heart. That alone is a great reason to feel joy!

God, thank You for all of Your blessings, especially those little ones that I forget about. Open my eyes to find joy all around me all the time. Amen.

Night 72
CHOOSING YOUR WORDS

"For it is by your words that you will not be guilty
and it is by your words that you will be guilty."

MATTHEW 12:37

✳

The words we say often come out of our mouths without
us thinking much about them. Words can be kind, like a
gentle spring rain; or they can cut like a sharp knife. Words
can stir things up or settle things down. Our words are so
important that Jesus spoke about them. Other people, who
can't see into our hearts, learn what's there by the way
we speak. Think about the words you said today. Were
they good and kind? Or maybe you need to apologize for
something you said.

Dear God, please help me to choose my words wisely.
I want each and every word that comes from my
mouth to be pleasing to You and to others. Amen.

Night 73
GOD'S COMMANDMENTS

"Do not steal."
EXODUS 20:15

✳

"Do not steal," the eighth of God's Ten Commandments, is one of the simplest to remember. Stealing can be more than just taking an item that belongs to someone else. If you think about it, there are other ways to steal. You can steal someone's place in line by being selfish and cutting in front of that person. You can steal a person's self-esteem by bullying them. You can steal someone's good character by saying bad things about them. God wants us not just to follow His commandments but also to really think about what they mean.

. . . .

Dear Father, help me to memorize and remember
Your Ten Commandments and not just know
them but also think about them. Amen.

Night 74
PEACE

Paul looked straight at the court and said,
"Brother Jews, I have lived for God with a heart
that has said I am not guilty to this day."

ACTS 23:1

What does it mean to have a clear conscience? It means that in your heart you know that what you did is right. When our hearts tell us we have done wrong, then we feel guilty. But knowing we have done right brings us peace. In Acts 24:16, Paul reminds us: always try to live so your heart says you are not guilty before God or man. What is your heart saying?

Help me, Lord, to live a clean life so that I can stand before You and others with a clear conscience. Amen.

Night 75
JESUS RESCUES

There is a way which looks right to a man,
but its end is the way of death.

PROVERBS 14:12

Often in a story, someone makes a wrong decision that gets him or her into trouble. This happens in real life too. We make decisions that can get us, and others, into a deep mess. But, just like in stories, we have a hero who comes to rescue us. It's Jesus! Jesus is the one who gets us out of our messes. We can count on Him to save us, no matter what. All we have to do is call on Him in prayer and then trust Him to arrive, at just the right time, to pull us up out of the mud and carry us safely in His arms.

Lord, come rescue me from the mess I'm in.
Lead me out of my frustration and fear.
I put my trust in You. I stand waiting,
knowing that You will save me. Amen.

Night 76
DON'T GIVE UP

My Christian brothers, you should be happy
when you have all kinds of tests. You know these
prove your faith. It helps you not to give up.

JAMES 1:2–3

Tonight's scripture comes from a letter written by James,
Jesus' oldest brother, to a group of Jewish Christians. James
told them not to give up. They had endlessly been made fun
of and punished for holding tightly to their faith, and they
were tired and worn out. God's encouraging us through the
words of James. When we're tired and beaten down with
our own problems and tests, we can be happy just knowing
that God is right there with us. God promises that He will
never leave or abandon us. All He asks is that we hold tightly
to our faith and not give up.

Father God, when I face hard times,
please strengthen my faith. Show me
Your mercy, gentleness, and love. In You
I find pure joy, and I praise You! Amen.

Night 77

A PROMISE YOU CAN COUNT ON

"Return to Me, and I will return
to you," says the Lord of All.

MALACHI 3:7

The people of Israel had wandered far from God and faced
all kinds of trouble. Sadly, they continued to sin. God chose
Malachi to deliver His final message to the people before
Jesus came. Malachi warned the people of Israel about their
sin. But he also reminded them of the love of their heavenly
Father. "Return to Me, and I will return to you." These words
from God were a promise to the people of ancient Israel, but
they are also for us. It is a promise we can always count on.

Whenever I stray from You, Lord, I feel empty
and alone. So many times, I've returned and
asked Your forgiveness, and always You've
loved me. Thank You, God! Amen.

Night 78
STRONG ROOTS

As you have put your trust in Christ Jesus the Lord to save you from the punishment of sin, now let Him lead you in every step. Have your roots planted deep in Christ. Grow in Him. Get your strength from Him. Let Him make you strong in the faith as you have been taught. Your life should be full of thanks to Him.

COLOSSIANS 2:6–7

How do we plant our roots deep in Jesus? First, we remember that Jesus lives in our hearts. Second, remember that strong roots run deep. Next, we believe what we have learned about Jesus in the Bible and what we have been taught by others. Finally, we give thanks to God. That's how we plant our roots deep in Jesus. He guides us through prayer and study, the fellowship of others, and practicing daily gratitude.

Guide me, Lord. Strengthen the roots of my faith. Lead me to those who will teach me Your ways, and then, Lord, keep me mindful of what I have learned. Amen.

Night 79
DO YOU HAVE WISDOM?

Happy is the man who does not walk in the way
sinful men tell him to, or stand in the path of
sinners, or sit with those who laugh at the truth.

PSALM 1:1

Following Jesus means having wisdom. And wisdom is available from God to everyone just by asking for it; however, not everyone chooses to make wise decisions. Sometimes it's easier to just go along with the crowd. This might take pressure off us and make us feel better in the moment. Later, though, we realize what we have done and how we have pushed ourselves away from God. The next time you are tempted to follow the crowd, be wise and remember the words of Psalm 1:1. Be happy. Do the right thing!

I am happy, God, when my actions please You.
But if I give in and follow the crowd, forgive
me. Thank You for second chances. Amen.

Night 80
GOD'S BETTER PLANS

Then Jesus turned to Peter and said,
"Get behind Me, Satan! You are standing in
My way. You are not thinking how God thinks.
You are thinking how man thinks."

MATTHEW 16:23

✳

Jesus spoke these sharp words, but He was right. God had a wonderful plan far beyond what Peter, or any human, could understand. Peter was about to do the wrong thing and get in Jesus' way of carrying out God's plan. We can get in the way of His plans for us too when we carelessly go our own way and do our own thing. It's so important not to act without talking with God first. He knows everything that's happening in our lives and each new step we should take.

Jesus, if I get in Your way, please stop me.
Help me to remember that Your thinking and
plans are so much greater than mine. Amen.

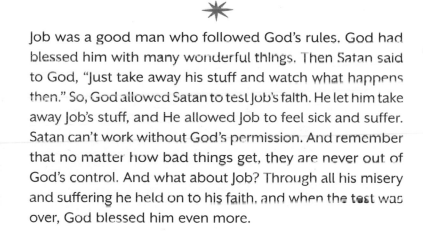

Night 81
GOD'S ALWAYS IN CONTROL

Then the Lord said to Satan, "See, all that he has is in your power. Only do not put your hand on him." So Satan went out from the Lord.

JOB 1:12

Job was a good man who followed God's rules. God had blessed him with many wonderful things. Then Satan said to God, "Just take away his stuff and watch what happens then." So, God allowed Satan to test Job's faith. He let him take away Job's stuff, and He allowed Job to feel sick and suffer. Satan can't work without God's permission. And remember that no matter how bad things get, they are never out of God's control. And what about Job? Through all his misery and suffering he held on to his faith, and when the test was over, God blessed him even more.

When I ask, "Why do bad things happen to good people?" God, remind me that You are always in control and You love me. Amen.

Night 82
GOOD ENOUGH!

*Who then can say we are guilty? It was Christ
Jesus Who died. He was raised from the dead.
He is on the right side of God praying to Him for us.*

ROMANS 8:34

Have you ever thought, *I'm not good enough*? Or maybe
someone hurt you and crushed your self-esteem? Well,
there's good news! You *are* good enough. When Jesus died
on the cross, He took your sins away. You are forgiven for
whatever you have done, and you don't have to carry any
guilt in your heart. Jesus is in heaven with God, praying for
you and helping you. So cheer up! Let Jesus lift your spirits.
He is always on your side.

If I don't feel good enough, Jesus, You lift
me up. If others say I'm not good enough,
You are on my side. Lord, You are my
treasured friend, and I love You. Amen.

A HUMBLE, GENTLE KING

"If anyone asks you, 'Why are you doing that?' say,
'The Lord needs it. He will send it back again soon.' "

MARK 11:3

✳

Jesus was about to enter the city of Jerusalem to celebrate
the Jewish festival of Passover. The people eagerly awaited
Him—the Messiah, the one who would save them. Jesus
told His disciples to borrow a young donkey so He could sit
on its back when He entered the city. Everything on earth
belonged to God. Jesus could have taken His Father's donkey,
but He borrowed and then returned it. Jesus was the great
King of kings, but He never acted like a wealthy, greedy king.
He was humble and gentle and always did the right thing.

Dear God, help me to remember that everything
I have is Yours. Remind me to share what I have
and to give back what I borrow. Amen.

Night 84
TRUE AND TRUSTWORTHY

Now in the city of Susa where the king
lived there was a Jew whose name was
Mordecai. . . . He had brought up. . .Esther, the
daughter of his father's brother. For she did not have
a father or mother. . . . When her father and mother
died, Mordecai took her as his own daughter.

ESTHER 2:5, 7

The book of Esther, in the Old Testament, is the true story
of a young queen, her cousin Mordecai, and how she saved
his life. Do you know that every story in the Bible is true?

Over and over again, the Bible is shown to be true and
trustworthy. Archaeological finds prove that people in the
Bible really existed and the events told about in the Bible
really happened. Second Timothy 3:16 says that everything
in the Bible comes from God. And we know that God does
not lie. We can always trust that His Word, the entire Bible,
is 100 percent true.

Father, how exciting it is to know that all the
stories I read in the Bible really happened! Amen.

Night 85
LIKE A LITTLE CHILD

He said, "For sure, I tell you, unless you have a
change of heart and become like a little child, you
will not get into the holy nation of heaven."

MATTHEW 18:3

Jesus said that everyone, young and old, needs to behave in
a similar way. We should depend on God for everything and
notice all the good things He puts around us in the world.
We should never think that we will be greater than anyone
else. Jesus told His disciples that instead of worrying about
being the greatest here or in heaven, they should change
their attitudes and think with the pure heart of a little child.

Lord Jesus, if ever I feel like I'm better
than anyone else, help me to remember
Your words in Matthew 18:3. Amen.

Night 86
ASKING FOR THE IMPOSSIBLE

Elijah said to Elisha, "Ask what I should do for you before I am taken from you." And Elisha said, "I ask you, let twice the share of your spirit be upon me."

2 KINGS 2:9

God was about to take Elijah up to heaven. But, just before that happened, Elijah asked Elisha what he could do for him. Elisha could have asked for anything. But he asked to become a prophet like Elijah and carry on God's work. It seemed an impossible request, but God allowed it to happen! He made Elisha the prophet who took Elijah's place. What might God give you if you asked for the impossible? God loves you. If your heart lines up with His plans for you, He might surprise you.

Lord, when I ask for what seems impossible, I know You will provide what is best for me. Whatever Your answer, I know that You love me. Amen.

COURAGE TO SHARE JESUS

Do not be ashamed to tell others about what our Lord said, or of me here in prison. I am here because of Jesus Christ. Be ready to suffer for preaching the Good News and God will give you the strength you need.

2 TIMOTHY 1:8

Paul had suffered a lot for talking about the Lord. People who hated Jesus also hated him. But Paul never gave up. He knew that all his suffering was worth it if it caused people to believe in Jesus so they could go to heaven. If anyone makes fun of you for talking about Jesus, don't you give up either! Remember Paul's words to Timothy. Keep spreading the good news about Jesus so others will believe and go to heaven someday. Trust God to give you the courage to share Jesus' story.

Lord, lead me to never be afraid to
tell others about Jesus. Amen.

Night 88
GOD KNOWS WHAT HE'S DOING

*He has made everything beautiful in its time.
He has put thoughts of the forever in man's
mind, yet man cannot understand the work
God has done from the beginning to the end.*

ECCLESIASTES 3:11

Everything God makes and does is perfect in His sight—even if it looks imperfect in ours. What we humans might see as ugly or broken or unfinished is just the way God wants it right now. Sometimes it's hard to find beauty in everything. But we need to remember that God's mind is so much greater than our own. And His timing isn't like ours. What we think needs to be fixed right now, God might not fix for months or years—or ever—on this earth. He always knows what He's doing, and He loves us.

God, I have so many unanswered questions
about life and about You. There are things I don't
understand. But I know this: You love me. Amen.

GOD HOLDS EVERYTHING TOGETHER

Christ was before all things.
All things are held together by Him.
COLOSSIANS 1:17

Imagine Jesus, in heaven now, holding our world together. It's not that He wraps His arms around our universe to keep it from falling apart. Instead, Jesus makes sure that everything in the universe is working perfectly. Earth's distance from the sun is perfect. Too cold or too hot means no life. Even our moon makes life possible by stabilizing the tilt of earth's axis. Astronomers are also discovering how other planets in our solar system help earth. Jesus holds it all together. Isn't it amazing that with all He has to do, He holds on to you too and cares about everything you do?

Jesus, I love You! I can't imagine how You hold everything in the universe together and still have time to take care of me all night and all day. Amen.

Night 90
WHAT DO YOU SEE?

"I looked at them with joy when they were
not sure of themselves, and the light
of my face gave them comfort."

JOB 29:24

Our bodies and actions often show what is going on inside us. Job must have been happy inside. His smile lit up his friends' lives. It made them feel comfortable with Job, and it brought some sunshine into their troubled lives. Look at yourself in the mirror. What do you see? Are you someone who smiles often, or do you keep your smiles to yourself? A smile, a gentle hug, an act of kindness, or a silent prayer might be just what someone needs. How can you share some sunshine?

Remind me, Jesus, to love others through my actions. A warm smile, a simple act of kindness, or a loving hug might be just what someone needs. Remind me, please. Amen.

Night 91
THE GOOD SHEPHERD

"My sheep hear My voice and
I know them. They follow Me."

JOHN 10:27

✳

Sheep graze in large flocks. They often spread out to find
the best spot for some tasty grass or cool water to drink.
They wander down ditches and ruts unaware of dangers
such as deep holes and wild animals. People are often like
sheep. We wander away from God, looking for what we
want and ignoring the dangers. And we also have a Good
Shepherd—Jesus—to watch over us and call us to safety. If
we listen, we can hear His voice even when we drift away.
Jesus wants us to hear and follow Him. Open your ears to
the Good Shepherd's voice. He will keep you out of trouble.

Lord, open my ears to hear You. Shout to me over the
noise of the world. Whisper to me in the darkness.
Lead me away from trouble and keep me safe. Amen.

Night 92
BE LIKE MOSES

But Moses said to the Lord, "See, the people of Israel
have not listened to me. How then will Pharaoh
listen to me? I am not able to speak well."

EXODUS 6:12

You would think God would choose a confident, sure-of-
himself person to lead. But Moses wasn't all that sure. Words
didn't come easy for him. Still, God chose Moses to lead.
And a great leader he was! Moses had a gift more important
than the gift of speaking well. His gift was listening to and
obeying God. Moses was faithful to God, and because of
that he bravely led the Israelites out of slavery. Maybe in
some ways you are not sure of yourself. You might think
there are things you can't do. Be like Moses! Listen to God.
Obey Him, and He will help you do great things.

Heavenly Father, I'm not always sure of my ability to do
the things You want me to do. Help me to get strength
from You. Keep me from getting in my own way. Amen.

Night 93
POWERFUL WORDS

Watch your talk! No bad words should be coming from your mouth. Say what is good. Your words should help others grow as Christians.

EPHESIANS 4:29

Words have power! They can build people up or tear them down. They can lead people toward doing something good or guide them to doing wrong. Words can help others trust God or make them think God does not exist. Ephesians 4:29 reminds you to choose your words wisely. Be careful what you say. Try to always use words that are gentle and kind. Delete all the bad words from your vocabulary. Speak words that please God and show others what it means to be a Christian.

Dear God, I don't often think about my words. Thank You for reminding me. I want everything I say to please You. Amen.

Night 94
FILTERING OUT THE BAD STUFF

How can a young man keep his
way pure? By living by Your Word.

PSALM 119:9

Imagine an aquarium filled with beautiful fish. The water is always clean because it passes through a filter that takes out all the bad stuff, like uneaten fish food and fish waste. The fish happily go on their way swimming around in clean water. But if it weren't for that filter, their water would be filthy and the fish not so happy. We are kind of like those fish, and we can think of God's Word, the Bible, as our filter. As you think about and put into action God's Word, you build up your filter and keep all the bad stuff away. That's how you keep your way pure!

Lord, teach me every day from Your Word.
Help me to learn from the Bible and to
live a pure and clean life. Amen.

Night 95
THE HOLY SPIRIT

No person who has become a child of God keeps
on sinning. This is because the Holy Spirit is in him.
He cannot keep on sinning because God is his Father.

1 JOHN 3:9

Accepting Jesus into our hearts doesn't mean that we stop
sinning. Every human sins. But the Holy Spirit is the one who
reminds us to do our best not to sin. And the Holy Spirit also
reminds us that Jesus died so we can be forgiven when we
do sin. The Holy Spirit is like our conscience. It is God's way
of speaking to us about our sin and helping us to do what is
right. Some people refer to the Holy Spirit as *that little voice
inside me.* Even when you do sin, you never have to worry
about being kicked out of God's family. You are His child. He
made you, and He loves you just the way you are—forever!

Dear Father, help me not to give in to sin.
And when I do sin, thank You for forgiving
me—Your gift to me through Jesus. Amen.

Night 96
GOD'S GREATNESS

When I look up and think about Your heavens, the work of Your fingers, the moon and the stars, which You have set in their place. . .

✳

Almost three thousand years ago, King David looked at the clear night sky. He gazed at the moon and stars and thought about God's greatness. He wondered how someone so wonderful and creative could care about him. In the summer of 1969, another man wondered the same thing. American astronaut Edwin "Buzz" Aldrin saw the night sky from the surface of the moon. As he stood on the moon's surface and gazed at the sky, he remembered the words of David, written in the King James Version of the Bible in Psalm 8:3–4. Three thousand years apart, two different men looked up at the sky—and they saw the same God.

* *

God, You are so great and yet You care for me! I love You. Amen.

Night 97
GOD'S FAMILY

You will know how to live in the family of God.

1 TIMOTHY 3:15 NCV

✦

Family is more than relatives. There is another family that you belong to, the family of God. When you asked Jesus to come into your heart, you became part of His family. You have many Christian brothers and sisters here on earth. Can you name other people you know who believe in Jesus? Your Christian family members and friends are your family of God. As you share the Bible together and discuss God and Jesus, you learn things like joy, courage, forgiveness, unselfishness, and love! Did you know that you can invite others into God's family? Pray and ask God to show you who needs to know Him.

Lord, lead me to those who need You.
Open my heart to welcome them into
my own family and Yours. Amen.

Night 98
WELCOMING UNBELIEVERS

Have loving-kindness for those who doubt.

JUDE 1:22

How does God want you to treat those who don't believe? Jesus is the best example of loving-kindness. He was kind to everyone, whether they believed or not. Even when unbelievers sent Him to die on the cross, Jesus prayed and said, "Father, forgive them. They do not know what they are doing" (Luke 23:34). What an awesome example of kindness! They wanted Jesus dead, and yet He prayed and asked God to forgive them. God wants you to treat everyone with loving-kindness too. Never be afraid to talk about Jesus when anyone asks why you are so kind. Maybe knowing you will turn their doubting into believing.

Heavenly Father, Jesus welcomed unbelievers, and He led them to You. I want to be like Jesus. Show me how to change doubt into faith and trust in You. Amen.

Night 99
WHO IS YOUR NEIGHBOR?

"Love your neighbor as yourself."
LEVITICUS 19:18

God wants us to love Him more than anyone and anything. He wants to be our one and only God all the time. God wants us to love ourselves too because He made us. Then God wants us to share all that love with our neighbors. Who are your neighbors? *Everyone* is your neighbor! Every man, woman, and kid in the world! Go spread some love around. Get in the habit of doing something nice for someone every day.

Dear Jesus, thank You for teaching me the two most important commandments. I love God, and I want to love Him even more. Please help me to do that and also to be a kind and loving neighbor. Amen.

TRUE AND PERFECT LOVE

This is love! It is not that we loved God but that He loved us. For God sent His Son to pay for our sins with His own blood.

1 JOHN 4:10

No matter how full of love our hearts are for God, we can never love Him as much as He loves us! True and perfect love can only come from Him. It's a kind of love not found anywhere on earth. God loved us so much that He couldn't imagine living without us. He made a home for us in heaven so we could live with Him someday. But He knew we couldn't come to Him filled with sin—it isn't allowed in heaven. So, God sent Jesus, the Son He loved with all His heart, to suffer and die, so when we get to heaven we won't bring any sin with us. Could you allow someone you love to suffer and die to save someone else? That's real love! God's kind of love.

Dear God, I'm grateful for how much You love me! I love You too. Amen.

Night 101
GOD'S WAYS

"For as the heavens are higher than the
earth, so are My ways higher than your ways,
and My thoughts than your thoughts."

ISAIAH 55:9

God has given us intelligence and common sense, and He
wants us to use our brains to think through everyday problems and come up with solutions. We are not as wise as
God, however, and sometimes the solution to our problem
may be different from anything we can imagine on our own.
God knows best, and though we may feel sure that His way
won't work, we need to trust Him. God is so wonderful and
amazing that we can't even begin to understand His ways.

Father, sometimes You do things that I
don't understand, and then I discover that
it leads to something great. Thank You for
always knowing what's best! Amen.

Night 102
THINK. . .THEN SPEAK

*"I say to you, on the day men stand before God,
they will have to give an answer for every word
they have spoken that was not important."*

MATTHEW 12:36

How easy it is to speak without thinking! Yet Jesus reminds us that our words are powerful, and we will be held responsible for how we use them. When you read about Jesus in the Bible, you discover that every word He spoke was important. He spoke kind words, wise words, words that people have learned from and lived by for more than two thousand years. What would our world be like if we all talked like Jesus? Remember always to think before you speak. Do your best to speak words that are pleasing to God's ears.

. . . .

Jesus, every word You spoke had power and
purpose. Help me to use my words so that they
will always bring You glory and honor. Amen.

Night 103
STOP!

Keep your heart pure for out of it
are the important things of life.

PROVERBS 4:23

As you head toward your teen years, you will face peer pressure from friends at school. Maybe someone will try to get you to take drugs, drink alcohol, or steal. You know that these things are wrong. Still, there's a strong pull toward giving in to your friends just to stay on their good side. When you feel that pull, *stop!* Remember that God requires you to have a pure heart. That means avoiding sin as best you can. So keep your heart pure, live to please God, and don't give in to sin. Always stay true to God, and He will reward you.

. . . .

Father, please help me to do only what is good and
right and not give in to pressure from others. Amen.

Night 104
WHATEVER HAPPENS. . .

"When you pass through the waters, I will be with
you. When you pass through the rivers, they will
not flow over you. When you walk through the fire,
you will not be burned. The fire will not destroy you."

ISAIAH 43:2

This is a promise from God that when we face trouble in
our lives, He will not abandon us.

Isaiah 43:2 does not mean that our bodies won't ever get
hurt or sick and one day die; but Isaiah 43:2 isn't about our
bodies. It reminds us that God is with us in whatever trouble
we face. Nothing can change that. Whatever happens, God
will be with you forever.

Father, when I face trouble, I will put my faith in
You and believe that You are with me. Amen.

Night 105
SOULS THAT LOVE

He was hated and men would have nothing to do
with Him, a man of sorrows and suffering, knowing
sadness well. We hid, as it were, our faces from Him.
He was hated, and we did not think well of Him.

ISAIAH 53:3

Eight hundred years before Jesus was born, the prophet Isaiah
predicted that Jesus would take on the sins of the world to
save humans from sin. He described Jesus' last days, a time
when many people would hate Him and hang Him on a cross
to die. Those people who hated Jesus weren't meant to be
like that! Sin had twisted their lives. When you face unpleasant people, don't think badly about them. Remember that
inside them there is a soul that God loves. Pray for them to
know and love Jesus. Pray for them to allow Jesus into their
hearts so they will live happy lives.

God, in each unpleasant person,
there is a soul You love. Show me how
I can help them to love You. Amen.

Night 106
JESUS CARES

*"Is not this the son of the man who makes
things from wood? Is not Mary His mother?
Are not James and Joseph and Simon and Judas
His brothers? And are not all His sisters here?
Then where did He get all these things?"*

MATTHEW 13:55–56

✴

Imagine being a kid growing up with Jesus as your brother. His siblings didn't know Jesus was here to save the world from sin. And Jesus never sinned, not even once! He did everything perfectly. It must have been hard for Jesus' brothers and sisters to be His siblings, but Jesus understood. He knew what it was like to grow up in a human family, but He also knew what it was like to be God's perfect Son. Remember this: nothing happens in your family that Jesus doesn't understand. Pray for your family members. Ask Jesus to save them from their troubles. He cares about your family just as He did His own.

Jesus, You understand what it's like to be
part of a human family. I'm glad that You
know what it's like to be me! Amen.

BE PATIENT

I did not give up waiting for the Lord. And He
turned to me and heard my cry. He brought
me up out of the hole of danger.

PSALM 40:1–2

King David wrote this Bible verse about a time he was trapped
in trouble with no apparent way out. He cried to God to
rescue him. Then he waited. It took time for God to answer,
but He did. David probably learned patience while he waited
and wondered if God cared about the trouble he was in.
We humans sometimes find ourselves in some sort of mess,
and we pray hard for God to save us. He will. We just need
to be patient.

Help me to be patient with You, God. I know that You
will answer me when the time is just right. Amen.

Night 108
GOD'S UNCHANGING WORD

God's Word is living and powerful. . . .
It tells what the heart is thinking
about and what it wants to do.

HEBREWS 4:12

People change, technology changes, thoughts and ideas change. . .but the Word of the Lord, the Bible, does not change. It will be as up-to-date two thousand years from now as it was two thousand years ago! Think about it: right now, you can learn what God says about your life by reading the Bible and filling your mind with His words—exactly like the ancient Israelites and the people in Jesus' time did. The Bible is awesome! Reading it is sort of like traveling in a God-made time machine. You can be in the past and present, both at the same time!

Thank You for the Bible, Lord. Help me
to fill my heart with Your Word. Amen.

Night 109
LEADERS WHO CARE

*"Let the greatest among you be as the least.
Let the leader be as the one who cares for others."*

LUKE 22:26

Sometimes when you're wrong, you're *really* wrong. Don't worry. Even the world's great leaders mess up at times. God doesn't judge them for the honest mistakes they make. He wouldn't judge you for your mistake either. Jesus says in Luke 22:26: "Let the leader be as the one who cares for others." Being a leader doesn't mean you must rule big crowds or lead an army. It doesn't mean you have to be the best at everything. Jesus says that leaders are those who care for others. If you help out at home, school, in your church or community, then God thinks of you as a leader. So wherever you go, lead! Show others that you care.

Jesus, open my eyes to the needs of others,
and lead me to help wherever I can. Amen.

Night 110
DO MORE!

*"Whoever makes you walk a short way,
go with him twice as far."*

MATTHEW 5:41

Jesus said don't just go the minimum distance—be willing to go twice as far. In other words, do more than is required of you. Think of all God does for you. He gives you His blessings, forgiveness, and strength even in your toughest circumstances. He gives you much more than He has to, and He wants you to follow His example. Choose to forgive when someone mistreats you. If someone leaves a mess in your house, clean it up. Help people without thinking about what you will get in return. Pray for the people others ignore. Love the unlovable. When you do these things, you will surely please God.

* *

God, help me to willingly do more than is expected of me, for no other reason than to please You. Amen.

Night 111
JESUS FIRST

"If any man comes to Me and does not have much more love for Me than for his father and mother, wife and children, brothers and sisters, and even his own life, he cannot be My follower."

LUKE 14:26

In this Bible verse, Jesus says something like, "Love Me so deeply that your love for your family will seem small by comparison." And in Matthew 10:37, He says, "He who loves his father and mother more than Me is not good enough for Me. He who loves son or daughter more than Me is not good enough for Me." Jesus meant that He wants to come first in our lives. We need to love Him with all our heart before we can truly love our family members or anyone else. Loving Him works like a circle. The more we love Jesus, the more we can love others. . .and the more we love others, the more we show our love for Him.

Jesus, please fill me up with love for You. Then let Your love shine through me to others. Amen.

Night 112
GOD SINGS

"The Lord your God is with you, a Powerful One Who wins the battle. He will have much joy over you. With His love He will give you new life. He will have joy over you with loud singing."

ZEPHANIAH 3:17

✳

God shows His great love for us in many ways. This scripture reminds us that God's mighty power saves us. He gets so much happiness from us, His children, that He expresses His joy over us with singing! People sing back to God to honor Him. They sing hymns and praise songs. God has a song written just for you. . .your name is its title. And the composer, God Himself, sings your song over you as you go about life here on earth. Close your eyes. Can you imagine God singing to you? Lift up your voice and sing a song of praise!

O Lord, what an awesome thought—Your voice singing to me—my song. Open my ears to Your voice! Amen.

Night 113
DIRTY FEET

*Jesus answered him, "You do not understand
now what I am doing but you will later."*

JOHN 13:7

Jesus got up from the supper table and began washing the disciples' feet. Walking around in sandals all day, feet got very dirty. In Bible times, it was the custom for feet to be washed before dinner, but by servants—not Jesus! One of His disciples, Peter, said, "Jesus, why?" Jesus told Peter that he wouldn't understand until later what He was doing. Those who hated Jesus would treat Him like a slave, a servant, and Jesus would die to "wash away" our sins. Sometimes we say, "Why, God?" when we face hard times. We need to trust that God knows what He's doing. He has a good reason for everything.

"Why, God?" I ask that question, and Your voice whispers, "Trust Me. I have it all under control." I trust You, Father. It is enough that You know why. Amen.

Night 114
TRUSTING GOD'S PROMISES

But Moses said to the people, "Do not be afraid! Be strong, and see how the Lord will save you today. For the Egyptians you have seen today, you will never see again."

EXODUS 14:13

✳

God had promised to deliver the Israelites from the Egyptians, and Moses believed Him. God told Moses to hold his staff—his walking stick—over the water. Then, in an awesome display of power, God divided the sea. The Israelites walked to the other shore on dry land. But when Pharaoh's warriors followed, the walls of water collapsed, drowning the entire army! Moses acted bravely because he trusted in God's promise. As you read the Bible, you will find many promises God has made to us all. Just like Moses, you can trust God to keep every single one.

Father, show me the promises in Your Word. Set them in my mind and heart. When I face trouble, remind me of Moses and the Red Sea, and I will be fearless. Amen.

STRONGER IN FAITH

Christian brothers, I want you to know that what has happened to me has helped spread the Good News.

PHILIPPIANS 1:12

Long ago, Christians were mistreated, even tortured and killed, because of their faith in Jesus. Paul, author of the book of Philippians, was one of them. He was hurt by stones hurled at him. He was imprisoned and shipwrecked during his missionary journeys. As he boldly shared the gospel, Paul grew even stronger in his faith. After Jesus rose from the dead, He said to His disciples, "Go to all the world and preach the Good News to every person" (Mark 16:15). When we choose to follow Jesus, it is our duty to share the gospel proudly and without worry, the way Paul did. Who will you share Jesus with tomorrow?

Jesus, You've told me to share the gospel with the world. Where should I share it tomorrow? Lead me to someone who needs to know You. Amen.

BETTER WITH LOVE

A dish of vegetables with love is better
than eating the best meat with hate.

PROVERBS 15:17

In this verse, was Solomon really telling us to eat our veggies? No! He simply meant that everything is made better with love. Solomon understood the human need for love and friendship. Imagine a world without love. It would be like eating your most favorite food but tasting nothing. Love is like a secret ingredient that makes everything—even your least favorite veggie—taste better. Fill up on God's love. You can never have too much of it, and it always tastes good.

Heavenly Father, I love You with all my heart,
all my soul, and all my mind. Help me to love
You even more. In Jesus' name I pray, amen.

Night 117
DON'T BE AFRAID

For they all saw Him and were afraid. At once Jesus talked to them. He said, "Take hope. It is I, do not be afraid." He came over to them and got into the boat. The wind stopped. They were very much surprised and wondered about it.

MARK 6:50–51

The storm came quick and strong. Angry waves and wind nearly tipped over the boat. The fishermen in the boat held on, almost sure they were about to die. And then, the very Son of God appeared standing on the water! "It is I," He said. *Jesus!* He climbed into the boat, and everything became calm. The storm ended. The danger was gone. Imagine how those fishermen must have felt! This story in the Bible really happened, and Jesus continues to work the same way today. Trust Jesus to help you. He will never leave you alone in a storm.

Jesus, nothing can keep You from me—not fire, flood, storms, not even the deepest ocean. I trust You to help stop anything that stands in my way. Amen.

Night 118
BREAD FROM HEAVEN

The bread from heaven stopped on the day after they had eaten some of the food of the land. So the people of Israel no longer had bread from heaven. But they ate food of the land of Canaan during that year.

JOSHUA 5:12

For forty years while the Israelites wandered in the desert heading for the Promised Land, God miraculously provided "bread from heaven" for them to eat (Exodus 16:1–16). God's special bread continued to appear all around them while they went on their way. It even covered the ground when they camped! But the day after the Israelites ate the Passover meal in the Promised Land, the bread stopped coming. God had begun to provide for them in a different way—food that grew by natural means. God knows exactly what we need and when we need it—every day, all the time! Isn't He wonderful?

Thank You, God, for providing for me. You know my every need, and You fulfill it at the perfect time and through Your perfect will. I love You, Father. Amen.

Night 119
HAPPY *AND* SAD

"Those who have sorrow are happy,
because they will be comforted."

MATTHEW 5:4

How can you be happy and sad at the same time? When Jesus said these words, He was speaking to a large crowd. They didn't know yet that He would die and save them from sin. He was preparing them for what was about to happen. He would die on the cross, and those who loved Him would be sad. But then, when He rose from the dead, all those who believed would have forever life in heaven. And *that* would make them happy! In life, tears will come—but so will God's comfort. When we feel sad, we can be happy knowing that God is with us, loving us all the time.

Father God, when I feel sad and tears fall from
my eyes, I am blessed because You calm me
with Your forever, comforting love. Amen.

Night 120

SOMEONE WHO UNDERSTANDS

The God Who lives forever is the Lord, the One Who made the ends of the earth. He will not become weak or tired. His understanding is too great for us to begin to know.

ISAIAH 40:28

✦

Being a kid isn't always easy. Occasionally, there are days that you feel like no one understands you, but there is someone who *always* understands. That someone is God. He understands kids, teenagers, grown-ups, old people—everyone! How deeply He understands us is beyond anything we can begin to know. On those days when it seems like no one understands you, talk with God in prayer. In Isaiah 1:18, He says, "Come now, let us think about this together." God understands what you are going through, and He will help you to sort out anything that troubles you.

Dear God, there are days when I feel like no one understands me. But You do, God! You always understand. Please remind me of that and help me to find my way. Amen.

Night 121
THE IMPORTANCE OF LOVE

And now we have these three: faith and hope
and love, but the greatest of these is love.

1 CORINTHIANS 13:13

✦

Paul reminds us about the importance of love in our lives. He says, "Love does not give up. Love is kind. Love is not jealous. Love does not put itself up as being important. Love has no pride. Love does not do the wrong thing. Love never thinks of itself. Love does not get angry. Love does not remember the suffering that comes from being hurt by someone. Love is not happy with sin. Love is happy with the truth. Love takes everything that comes without giving up. Love believes all things. Love hopes for all things. Love keeps on in all things. Love never comes to an end" (1 Corinthians 13:4–8). And what is love? God! There is no greater love than God.

Dear God, please help my love for You
to grow stronger every day. Amen.

Night 122
BE STILL

Be quiet and know that I am God.
PSALM 46:10

Read about David in the Bible, and you will learn that he experienced a great deal of trouble. The only way he survived was by trusting in the Lord. David wrote in Psalm 4:4, "When you are on your bed, look into your hearts and be quiet." Remember that. As you close your eyes tonight, instead of tossing and turning, think about God and how wonderful He is. When you learn to trust that God can protect you and work out your problems, then you can lie down peacefully and sleep. "I will lie down and sleep in peace. O Lord," says David. "You alone keep me safe" (Psalm 4:8).

. . . .

Dear God, quiet my mind. Remove all the worldly thoughts that come between You and me. Create stillness inside me and turn my thoughts to You. Amen.

Night 123
A NEW HEART!

"I will give them one heart, and put a new spirit within them. I will take the heart of stone out of their flesh and give them a heart of flesh."

 EZEKIEL 11:19

We are all born needing a heart transplant of sorts. God wants to give us a good heart, a place worthy of Him to live in—a heart that is open and ready to see, hear, and love Him. The good news is that we received our heart transplant the day we believed Jesus died for us. His death saved us from sin. It created in us a heart that beats to please God, a heart that loves and does good and kind things. This new heart changes everything! It gives us a heart that will beat forever—now and someday in heaven.

Thank You, Lord, for giving me a new heart, a heart so perfect in love that it will last forever. Amen.

Night 124
GOD'S PERFECT TIMING

"God is not a man, that He should lie. He is not a son of man, that He should be sorry for what He has said. Has He said, and will He not do it? Has He spoken, and will He not keep His Word?"

NUMBERS 23:19

✳

God is perfect in every way. He is not sorry for anything He has said, because all of His words are right and true. Best of all, God keeps His promises. When He says that He will do something, He does it. God *always* keeps His word. Because God is not human, His timing is not the same as ours. God will wait for the perfect time to act, and what He does might be far beyond our understanding. That's what makes Him our great God—not human, but amazing and awesome—our God who loves and cares for us in every way.

Father, when I think of You in human terms,
remind me that You are God. Anything
is possible with You. Amen.

Night 125
FREE TREASURE

"I tell you this: Do not worry about your life.
Do not worry about what you are going to eat and
drink. Do not worry about what you are going to
wear. Is not life more important than food? Is
not the body more important than clothes?"

MATTHEW 6:25

✳

This is part of Jesus' Sermon on the Mount. As He spoke
to the huge crowd, Jesus taught about the cares of life. His
speech included five great ideas that—if followed—would
bring people inner peace. What if we turned our worries
away from our stuff and focused instead on God? What
would we be left with? Jesus said we would be left with a
treasure, one that never goes out of style! A treasure that
moths and rust can't destroy and thieves don't break in and
steal (Matthew 6:20). And the best part is. . .it's free! What we
are left with is God's love and everything that comes with it!

Heavenly Father, help those looking for
happiness in their things to see that You are
what they are searching for. Amen.

Night 126
JESUS FIXES BROKEN THINGS

The Lord is near to those who have a broken heart.
And He saves those who are broken in spirit.

PSALM 34:18

Imagine this: you are planning to run with your older brother in a marathon. Every day, for months, you train. Day by day you get stronger and stronger. And finally—you are ready. Race time. "Runners. On your mark. Get set. Go!" You and your brother take off running. And then, you fall and break your leg! But that isn't all that's broken. So is your heart. A doctor's help and time will fix your broken leg, but who will fix your broken heart? Jesus will! And you know you can count on Him.

I am never alone, God. When I feel sad,
You are with me. You care for me and comfort me.
Oh what a loving Father You are! Amen.

Night 127
MAKING GOD PROUD

I can have no greater joy than to hear that
my children are following the truth.

3 JOHN 1:4

Jesus' disciple John was happy to learn that the people he had taught to love Jesus (John called these people his children) were continuing to follow in Jesus' footsteps and spreading the gospel. Hearing this brought John great joy. Someone else loves hearing good things about His children. . .God! He loves hearing compliments about us, His kids. When you receive a compliment, imagine that it's coming right from the mouth of your heavenly Father. You are His child. Make Him proud with all that you do.

Dear God, I want everything I do to
make You proud of me. Amen.

Night 128
TEAMING UP WITH JESUS

"Take my yoke upon you and learn from me."
MATTHEW 11:29 NIV

✳

Jesus said, "Take my yoke upon you." To understand what He meant, you need to understand what a yoke is. A yoke is a wooden bar, or frame, that connects two oxen at the neck. It is used when the animals carry a heavy load. The yoke balances the load and makes it easier for them to carry. Taking Jesus' yoke means coming to Him and accepting His help. When you team up with Jesus, then He teaches you how to handle any heavy problem that comes your way. Think about Jesus' words in Matthew 11:30. He says, "For My way of carrying a load is easy and My load is not heavy."

* *

Jesus, sometimes I try to carry the load all by myself.
I forget that teaming up with You makes the burden
light. Together, we can do anything! Amen.

Night 129
DO YOU CHOOSE JESUS?

Pilate wanted to please the people. He gave
Barabbas to them and had Jesus beaten. Then
he handed Him over to be nailed to a cross.

MARK 15:15

✳

Pilate didn't want anything to do with this Jesus fellow.
Even Pilate's wife warned him not to get involved. So, he
stalled. . .and then decided to release Barabbas, a murderer,
and kill Jesus, an innocent man. Was Pilate an all-around bad
guy? No. He decided to please the crowd. Most of the time,
it's fun to be in big groups. Usually they're harmless, and
because of that it's often okay to go with the flow. But when
the crowd laughingly suggests something that makes you
uncomfortable, ask yourself: Are you choosing the wrong
way, or are you choosing Jesus?

I choose You, Jesus! When the crowd presses in
around me trying to pull me away from You and
Your teaching, Jesus, I choose You! Amen.

Night 130
A GLIMPSE OF HEAVEN

*Before the throne there was what looked like a
sea of glass, shining and clear. Around the throne
and on each side there were four living beings
that were full of eyes in front and in back.*

REVELATION 4:6

God allowed John a brief glimpse into heaven, and what he
saw there amazed him. Four creatures surrounded God's
throne, almost like the stately lions some kings kept chained
near theirs—only these beasts were unchained and far more
majestic! God also allowed the prophet Ezekiel a peek at
these creatures. Ezekiel called them cherubim and described
them as having humanlike bodies (Ezekiel 1:5; 10:1). These
incredible heavenly beings are proof of God's creativity. Who
knows what awaits us when we get to heaven? Certainly, it
will be unlike anything we have seen here on earth.

God, Your creativity is beyond my imagination.
I wonder what incredible things I will
see someday in heaven. Amen.

Night 131
GROWING STRONG

Growing strong in body is all right but growing in God-like living is more important. It will not only help you in this life now but in the next life also.

1 TIMOTHY 4:8

✳

Imagine this: What if God allowed Paul, the Bible's letter writer, to visit earth for a day? Paul walks into a gym and says to a man nearby, "Growing strong in body is all right but growing in God-like living is more important. It will not only help you in this life now but in the next life also." In ancient times, Paul understood that growing as a Christian is more important than growing a strong body. When you live a Christian life and follow Jesus, He will make you strong in character. Growing strong in your body is good, but Jesus makes you strong in *every* way!

Jesus, I am a Christian in training. You have given me all the training equipment I need: Your Word, prayer, and faith in You. Thank You! Amen.

Night 132
THE HELPER

"The Helper is the Holy Spirit. The Father will send
Him in My place. He will teach you everything and
help you remember everything I have told you."

JOHN 14:26

Jesus' time on earth was about to end and—in tonight's verse—
He prepared His disciples for His departure. The disciples
were confused and afraid, so Jesus comforted them with
words of assurance, peace, and hope. He said, "Do not let
your hearts be troubled or afraid" (v. 27).

And Jesus promised them that He would send the Father's
Helper, the Holy Spirit, to teach, direct, guide, and remind
them of every word He had told them. Through His presence inside us, we learn to know God. The Helper comforts
us and helps us to understand the Bible. Because the Holy
Spirit lives in our hearts, we are never ever alone!

Helper, Strengthener, Comforter, Adviser,
Counselor, Friend—oh, Holy Spirit of God!
Thank You for living in my heart, guiding me,
and drawing me near to God. Amen.

Night 133
DANGEROUS SITUATIONS

Even though I walk through the darkest valley,
I will fear no evil, for you are with me; your
rod and your staff, they comfort me.

PSALM 23:4 NIV

Sheep traveled into valleys for food and water, but the valley also contained danger. The shepherd was prepared, though. Using his tall staff with a crooked end, he could snare a sheep from a swamp or guide it in fast-moving waters. His rod, a short stick with leather strips on the end, kept the flies and mosquitoes away—and could be used in cleaning and grooming. Like sheep, we humans get into dangerous situations in the valleys of life. But the Lord stays with us, protects us, and saves us when we get into trouble.

Jesus, You are my shepherd. You direct me where I should go, steer me from danger, and rescue me when I stray. You never leave me, and I am so grateful. Amen.

Night 134
WHEN YOU DOUBT

"The blind are made to see. Those who could not walk are walking. Those who have had bad skin diseases are healed. Those who could not hear are hearing. The dead are raised up to life and the Good News is preached to poor people."

MATTHEW 11:5

✳

John the Baptist had always believed that Jesus was the Son of God, our Savior. Everywhere he went, John preached about Jesus. And it got him into trouble. When John told King Herod about Jesus, it made the king angry. He had John thrown into prison. Chained to a prison wall, John needed reassurance from Jesus. He sent a message: "Are You the one who was to come?" Jesus replied: "The blind see. The lame walk. Skin diseases are healed. The deaf hear. The dead are raised up to life." If you doubt, then remember Jesus' answer to John. Everything He did, *all the miracles*, were real. And Jesus is still with us today, in Spirit, helping us in every way.

• •

Jesus, when I doubt, remind me of the great miracles You performed. Amen.

Night 135
RULES FOR A GOOD LIFE

"Keep these words in your heart that I am telling you today. Do your best to teach them to your children. Talk about them when you sit in your house and when you walk on the road and when you lie down and when you get up."

DEUTERONOMY 6:6–7

God is speaking in this verse, and the words He wants us to keep in our hearts are the Ten Commandments.

Put God first. He should be your one-and-only God.
Worship God only.
Be respectful when using God's name.
Remember the Sabbath.
Respect your parents.
Do not kill.
Be faithful to the one you marry.
Do not steal.
Do not lie.
Do not be jealous of what others have.

These are God's rules for living a good Christian life.

God, I will remember Your Ten Commandments and do my best to obey them. Amen.

Night 136
ALL GOD'S CHILDREN

Jesus said, "Who is My mother?
And who are My brothers?"
MATTHEW 12:48

✸

With these words, Jesus was expanding the definition of family. He said, "Whoever does what My father in heaven wants him to do is My brother and My sister and My mother" (v. 50). Jesus was reminding the crowd that we are all God's children. When we accept Jesus as our Savior, God adopts us into His forever family and promises us a place in heaven. When we remember that we are all God's kids, then it becomes easier to lend a helping hand to strangers, like a new kid at school or a kid no one likes, or a person in your neighborhood. Who, in God's family, can you help?

I am honored to be a member of Your family, God.
How can I help my sisters and brothers? Amen.

Night 137
TEST OF FAITH

Later God tested Abraham, and said to him,
"Abraham!" Abraham said, "Here I am."

GENESIS 22:1

✳

Then God said to Abraham, "Take. . .your only son, Isaac,
whom you love. . . . Give him as a burnt gift on the altar
in worship" (Genesis 22:2). What? Was God *really* telling
Abraham to allow his son to be killed as an offering? Still,
Abraham obeyed God. He trusted God to bring Isaac back
to life. He was ready to follow God's command. God did
not allow Abraham to sacrifice his son. But it was a test of
Abraham's faith. And Abraham passed God's test. He was
ready to trust God with everything—even his beloved son.
Remember this: God will never give you a test that is beyond
your ability to pass.

Father God, if You decide to test me, then give
me the strength and courage to pass Your test.
Build my faith. Make it strong. Amen.

Night 138
THE LIVING WORD

All the Holy Writings are God-given and are made alive by Him. Man is helped when he is taught God's Word. It shows what is wrong. It changes the way of a man's life. It shows him how to be right with God.

2 TIMOTHY 3:16

The Bible is as reliable today as it ever was! Scripture speaks to us in our current situations just as it did to people a few thousand years ago. . .and just as it will forever. God's Word helps us to know right from wrong. It is a powerful teacher. Everything changes throughout history, but God has been able to speak to people exactly where they are through His living Word. There is certainly no other book or any other thing in the world that can do that. Only the living Word, the Bible, continues to be God-breathed and up-to-date forever.

Dear God, all things pass into history except for You and Your Word. How wonderful it is that Your Word will live forever! Amen.

Night 139
A HEAVENLY CELEBRATION

The death of His holy ones is of great worth in the eyes of the Lord.

PSALM 116:15

✳

We all will die one day. We don't know when or how, but God does. And He does not want us to worry about it or to be afraid. He wants us to wake up every morning expecting to live a long and happy life. Death should be the furthest thing from a kid's mind, except for one thing—to remember that when we die, our souls keep on living in heaven with God forever. When a person dies, loved ones feel sad because that person is gone. But, at the same time, there is a great celebration in heaven. God celebrates being with His beloved child. Focus your thoughts on how much God loves you and be happy that you will be with Him someday.

Lord, I am not just my body. My soul lives within it with You, and after my body dies, I know I will live on in heaven as Your precious child. Amen.

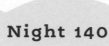

Night 140
GOD, HELP!

There was no king in Israel in those days.
Each man did what he thought was right.

JUDGES 21:25

✳

The ancient Israelites bounced from one disaster to another while ignoring God's Law. They only shaped up when they faced an enemy—then they cried out to God for help. We are a lot like those ancient Israelites. Too often we do what is right in our own eyes. We give in to temptation and sin, and that gets us into trouble. Then we cry out to God, "Help! Get me out of this mess!" Ignoring God's rules didn't work for the Israelites, and it won't work for us today. It is wise to examine what we think of as right and wrong. Ask yourself, "Whose rules am I following?" Then do your best to follow God's rules.

I don't want to be separated from You, Lord,
by going my own way. Remind me, please,
to check what I think is right and wrong and
make sure I'm following Your rules. Amen.

Night 141
SHARING GOD'S WORD

Until I come, read and preach and
teach the Word of God to the church.

1 TIMOTHY 4:13

✳

The Bible is a book that should be shared with others. It was never meant to only be read in silence. When God's Word is shared aloud, it gives people a chance to discuss what God is saying and to learn from one another. Maybe you only hear God's Word spoken in church and Sunday school. Those are good places to share His Word, but you should also be sharing the Bible with your family and friends. Get in the habit of reading the Bible aloud. Listen to its words and imagine yourself in the situations God's people faced long ago. Then think about what those words mean to you.

Dear God, I don't often think about reading the Bible aloud. Thank You for reminding me to do that. Amen.

Night 142
CHANGE OF HEART

*I pray that your hearts will be able to understand.
I pray that you will know about the hope given by
God's call. I pray that you will see how great the things
are that He has promised to those who belong to Him.
I pray that you will know how great His power is.*

EPHESIANS 1:18–19

✴

This scripture is part of Paul's letter to his church friends. In it, he prays for their hearts to understand about God. Years before, God had made Paul blind—that was when Paul, then known as Saul, hated Jesus. But afterward, Jesus miraculously healed Paul. Not only did Paul receive a change of heart, but his eyes were literally opened to Jesus (Acts 9:1–19). Your heart is important not only for your physical life but for your spiritual life as well. It's the part of your soul containing all your thoughts, delights, and wants. Paul wanted his friends to experience what he had—a trusting heart filled with the love of Jesus.

Father, please open my heart to
understand more about You. Amen.

Night 143
GOD SEES

Do not let yourselves get tired of doing good.
If we do not give up, we will get what
is coming to us at the right time.

GALATIANS 6:9

In today's Bible verse, Paul is reminding his friends not to be discouraged that their hard work went unrewarded. His friends had been telling everyone they met about Jesus. And often, their message was met with hatred. These Jesus followers were doing their best to be kind and to do good works, and they got nothing good in return. Paul told them not to give up and that God would reward them when the time was just right. Learn from Paul. Don't give up trying when no one seems to notice the good work you've done. God knows, and He will bless you! And remember to thank the people who are kind and work hard for you.

God, help me to never stop doing good work,
even if I'm discouraged, and remind me to
thank those who are kind to me. Amen.

Night 144
A GOOD, GOOD FATHER

The Lord has loving-pity on those who fear Him, as a father has loving-pity on his children. For He knows what we are made of. He remembers that we are dust.

PSALM 103:13–14

God is our Father. He understands that humans, young and old, sin sometimes. They mess up and worry that God might be angry and not forgive them. But they don't need to be afraid! God made each of us. He knows all about us. He knows when we sin. He knows when we're sorry. And God will always have loving-pity on us—His kids. When we confess our sin and ask for His forgiveness, He wipes away our sin like it never happened. What a wonderful heavenly Father we have!

Heavenly Father, I am not afraid to confess my sins to You, because I know You will look on me with loving-pity and forgive me. Amen.

Night 145
LISTEN MORE THAN YOU SPEAK

My Christian brothers, you know everyone
should listen much and speak little. He should
be slow to become angry. A man's anger
does not allow him to be right with God.

JAMES 1:19–20

✳

Many teachers of the New Testament believe that James,
the writer of these verses, was Jesus' half brother. Most of
the time when Jesus spoke, people listened. But there were
some, even leaders of the church, who closed their ears
to His teaching and talked—a lot!—about themselves. And
James had probably seen how angry some people were with
his brother. They hated Jesus for no reason other than He
said He was the Son of God. James learned from his brother
to be wise about listening and about not becoming angry.
Read his words aloud. Listen and let them sink deep into
your heart.

Jesus, sometimes I talk when I should be listening.
Teach me to be quiet and to learn from You. Amen.

Night 146
KEEP ON FORGIVING

Then Peter came to Jesus and said, "Lord, how many times may my brother sin against me and I forgive him, up to seven times?" Jesus said to him, "I tell you, not seven times but seventy times seven!"

MATTHEW 18:21–22

✳

Jesus' disciple Peter asked Jesus a simple question: "How many times do I need to forgive someone?" We wonder what was in Peter's head when he asked this question. Did he want others to admire his generosity at being willing to forgive seven times? Whatever Peter's reason for asking, Jesus' answer was probably not what Peter expected. Jesus answered, "Not seven times, but seventy times seven!" In other words, *keep on forgiving*! God forgives us for every sin we confess to Him. Think about how many times we sin in a lifetime. That's generous forgiving, and that's how God wants us to forgive others.

Lord, my heart holds tightly to hurt feelings.
But You have given me the ability to forgive
even the worst of sins. Thank You. Amen.

Night 147

PRAISE INSTEAD OF COMPLAIN

Even if the fig tree does not grow figs and there is no fruit on the vines, even if the olives do not grow and the fields give no food. . .yet I will have joy in the Lord. I will be glad in the God Who saves me.

HABAKKUK 3:17–18

✳

Habakkuk was tired of the tough times he lived in. And so he took his complaints to God. When would the trouble stop? Why hadn't God answered his prayers for help? God answered. Yes, He was aware of what was going on, and yes, He would help, but it would come about in His timing. Then Habakkuk's complaints switched to words of praise, which is amazing because nothing had changed. How is it possible that Habakkuk could praise God in the middle of such trouble? It's because he understood that joy is found in Jesus alone. Situations change, and people come in and out of lives; but Jesus is *always* with us, all the time, all the way.

Dear Jesus, thank You for being the only blessing I need. Amen.

Night 148
USING YOUR GIFTS

For this reason, I ask you to keep using the gift
God gave you. It came to you when I laid my hands
on you and prayed that God would use you.

2 TIMOTHY 1:6

✳

Some stuff we outgrow and give away, but we should never
allow God's gifts to be tucked away somewhere, unused.
God gives each of us certain talents—things we are good
at. They are His precious gifts to us, and we need to use
them. God wants us not only to use His gifts but also to
share them and do good with them. When we put God's
gifts into action to serve Him, God knows that He can trust
us with even more. His gifts to us will increase, strengthen,
and multiply. Are you using the gifts God has given you?
Can He trust you with even more?

God, You have given me special talents and inspiring
gifts. Open my eyes to sharing my gifts. Through faith
and obedience I will use them to serve You. Amen.

Night 149
LIVING FOR JESUS

No, Christian brothers, I do not have that life yet. But I
do one thing. I forget everything that is behind me and
look forward to that which is ahead of me. My eyes
are on the crown. I want to win the race and get the
crown of God's call from heaven through Christ Jesus.

PHILIPPIANS 3:13–14

After Saul met Jesus, who had been raised from the dead, on
a road leading to the city of Damascus, everything changed,
even his name. Saul became Paul, one of the greatest Jesus
followers ever. By the time Paul wrote the words in Philippians
3:13–14, he had put thoughts of his past sins behind him. He
focused only on serving God and the promise that one day
he would live in heaven. God forgives us for past sins, and
Paul reminds us not to dwell on what we've done. Instead,
we need to move on, living our lives for Jesus.

Father, allow me to focus on the present.
What can I do for You? How can I spread Your
Word where it is most needed right now? Amen.

Night 150
JESUS' EXAMPLE

*He went away again the second time. He prayed,
saying, "My Father, if this must happen to
Me, may whatever You want be done."*

MATTHEW 26:42

Jesus' prayers show us the 100 percent human side of Him. In
one of His darkest hours, Jesus was overwhelmed with human
emotions. He asked God for something that He would not
provide. But Jesus, perfect and obedient, ended His prayers
by saying, "May whatever You want be done." This is one
of those times when we read about Jesus and discover that
He had a human side that allowed Him to understand our
feelings. He knows how it feels when God says no. Do your
best to follow Jesus' example. Remember that God knows
best. When God says no to your prayers, focus on how much
He loves you—even when His plans don't match yours.

Father, I wonder why You refuse when I ask
for what I think is right. But Your knowledge is
greater than my understanding. So Your will be
done, God. . .Your perfect will be done. Amen.

A HELPING HAND

*If you know what is right to do
but you do not do it, you sin.*

JAMES 4:17

Today's world is very different from the way it was when Jesus lived. In His time, people were not as unsure about helping a stranger in need. Stepping in to help in a dangerous situation is heroic. But what about stepping in for the little stuff? How many times do we think, *It would be really nice if I did something for this person,* and then talk ourselves out of it? *They'll think this is silly. They won't even notice. I don't have time.* James reminds us to stay focused on doing what's right. We never know what the future holds. We never know when we might need a helping hand from someone else.

. . . .

Dear God, make me aware of little ways that I
can brighten the lives of others. Where You see
a need, Father, send me to fill it. Amen.

SERVING OTHERS

*"He who is greatest among you will
be the one to care for you."*

MATTHEW 23:11

"If I had a million dollars," a boy said, "I'd hire a butler." That sounded a bit selfish, so the boy said, "Everyone could have one!" "And whose butler would *you* be?" his father answered. "If everyone had a butler or maid, then that would include the butlers and maids! The only way everyone could be taken care of like that would be if all the people with servants also were servants!" Everyone taking care of everyone else—that's exactly what Christians are supposed to do. Jesus served us through His death and beyond. And God has already done everything for us by giving us this world, this life, and the next. Whose servant will you be?

. . . .

Jesus, I sometimes miss opportunities to serve
You and others. Open my heart to the possibilities.
Teach me to be a good servant. Amen.

Night 153
GOD'S SON

"You are My Son. Today I have become Your Father."
HEBREWS 5:5

✴

No one knows for sure who wrote the book of Hebrews in the Bible. But one thing is sure: its writer understood the power of God's Son, Jesus. The author of Hebrews wanted everyone to know that Jesus was a part of God from the very beginning. Just like God, Jesus always existed.

Some of the most important passages in the Bible are when Jesus talks to His Father (Luke 22:42; 23:34, 46). To a Roman soldier, the Man on the cross "was the Son of God" (Matthew 27:54). In the heart of every believer is the truth that Jesus is God's "only Son" (John 3:16).

The Bible teaches that, without a doubt, Jesus is God's Son. He has always been, and He is forever.

Son of God, You are so wonderful! How amazing that God sent You to save me from sin. Jesus, You are in my heart. I love You. I praise You. Amen.

GOD'S MIRACLES

"I sent the hornets ahead of you. They drove out the people and the two kings of the Amorites from in front of you. You did not do it by your sword or bow."

JOSHUA 24:12

✳

Throughout the book of Joshua, Israel's armies fought the Canaanites in one battle after another. You could certainly get the impression that their swords and bows had a lot to do with them taking Canaan, the Promised Land. But wait! Almost every battle came with a miracle: collapsing walls, hailstorms, prolonged daylight—even God inspiring them to go on night marches and launch surprise sunrise attacks. God did these miracles so Israel would understand that only *He* could give them victory and that they should respect and serve Him (Joshua 24:8–14; 2 Chronicles 20:12, 15). God still does miracles to help us reach our goals today!

• •

You are always present in life's big moments.
Thank You, God, for Your greatness and Your love. Amen.

Night 155
FAMILY HISTORY

Jesus was about thirty years old when He began His work. People thought Jesus was the son of Joseph, the son of Heli. Heli was the son of Matthat. Matthat was the son of Levi. Levi was the son of Melchi. Melchi was the son of Jannai. Jannai was the son of Joseph.

LUKE 3:23–24

Have you ever wondered why God included such long and boring family histories in the Bible? We need to remember that the Bible isn't just for us. It is a book for all humankind. And in some world cultures, a person hasn't been properly introduced until his or her family history is known. The Bible's long lists of ancestors aren't boring to the people in those countries. Instead, Jesus, Mary, and Joseph are shown in their proper family setting. Isn't it great that God thought of everyone when He gave the world the Bible?

Father, I think it's neat that You've included family history in the Bible. It reminds me that I have a long list of ancestors here on earth, but I am also a child of God! Amen.

Night 156
PRICELESS WORD OF GOD

"Heaven and earth will pass away,
but My words will not pass away."
MATTHEW 24:35

✳

If all the Bibles ever printed were still available, there would be one for every person alive today—with plenty left over. The New Testament has been translated into half of the world's languages. The Bible can be read in braille, downloaded from the internet, heard as audiobooks, and carried around in a cell phone. One hundred million copies are sold each year, and the average American home is estimated to contain four Bibles. Heaven and earth are still around, but some people still haven't read or believed in God's Word. Pray that they come to believe.

Jesus, Your words are priceless. I pray for everyone in the world to come to believe in them as the truth and receive Your gift of forever life in heaven. Amen.

Night 157
GOD'S GREAT MERCY

"We are not asking this of You because we are right
or good, but because of Your great loving-pity."

DANIEL 9:18

✴

God sees our good works. But nothing we do earns us His
blessings or even His forgiveness. Daniel understood this.
That's why when he prayed, asking God to get his people
out of trouble, Daniel asked God for loving-pity. Loving-pity
is the same as mercy. Mercy is when God doesn't punish
us for our sins as we deserve. Remember—Jesus took that
punishment for us. And God forgives all our sins as soon
as we ask. Let's join Daniel in understanding that we bring
absolutely nothing to God. But let's also know, like Daniel,
that in God's great mercy, He chooses to hear, love, and
forgive us.

Mighty God, Your great loving-pity is beyond
my understanding. I have nothing to bring You,
yet in my sinfulness You hear me, love me,
and forgive me. Thank You, Father. Amen.

Night 158
THE WHOLE TRUTH

But many came and told false things about Him.
At last two came to the front. They said, "This
Man said, 'I am able to destroy the house of
God and build it up again in three days.' "

MATTHEW 26:60–61

Have you ever played the telephone game? One person whispers something to the next person in line. That person passes it on. And by the time the message gets to the last person, it sounds entirely different! That's the kind of thing that went on in the final days of Jesus' life. False information was passed around. When Jesus said, "Destroy this house of God and in three days I will build it again" (John 2:19), He was talking about His body, His crucifixion, and His resurrection.

We need to be careful when quoting Jesus' words or any other words in the Bible. They are written just as they are because they are the true, perfect words of God.

. . . .

The Bible says add nothing to Your Word.
When sharing Your Word with others, God, may I
speak only Your words and Your truths. Amen.

Night 159
GOD HEARS

I love the Lord, because He hears
my voice and my prayers.

PSALM 116:1

Whether we are offering our praise to God or coming to Him with our troubles, we know from the few words in this verse that God hears us. Isn't that mind-blowing? The almighty God of the universe who created and put together every particle in existence hears us when we come to Him. Maybe we go to the Lord in song, praising Him. Maybe we spend some time reading and thinking about God's Word. Maybe we are praying to Him as we reach out for His comfort. Whatever we do, God hears us and is interested in what we have to say. Isn't that a great reason to love the Lord?

I have so many reasons to love You, God, so many reasons to worship and praise You. How grateful I am that You hear my voice! I love You, Lord. Amen.

Night 160
WHO SHOULD YOU TELL?

Herod was afraid of John. He knew he was a good
man and right with God, and he kept John from
being hurt or killed. He liked to listen to John
preach. But when he did, he became troubled.

MARK 6:20

John the Baptist's life was in King Herod's hands. Herod's wife
wanted John dead, so her husband threw him in prison and
later ordered him killed. John shouldn't have lived as long
as he did, but Herod liked to listen to him. Why? Because
there is a soul in each of us that pulls us toward God. A
tiny part of Herod must have hoped John would answer
his questions and show him the way to the Lord. Sadly,
it never happened. Herod was more concerned with his
kingly position. God wants us to reach the "godless." They
might struggle and fight against it—but their souls cry out to
be saved. Look around you. Who can you tell about Jesus?

Dear God, lead me to the godless ones You
know I can help. Give me the perfect words
and actions to lead them to You. Amen.

OPPOSITES

Do not be joined together with those who do
not belong to Christ. How can that which is
good get along with that which is bad? How can
light be in the same place with darkness?

2 CORINTHIANS 6:14

Paul asks us to think about opposites, like good and bad
and light and darkness. He reminds us that both cannot exist
in the exact same place at the same time. Imagine yourself
sitting in a dark room. If someone turns on a light, the whole
atmosphere of the room changes. That's what it's like for a
nonbeliever to believe! Jesus comes into that person's heart
and lights it up with His love. Everything changes—for the
better! Paul warns us not to be joined together with nonbelievers. We need to be careful so they don't pull us away
from Jesus.

I know it's possible for nonbelievers to turn
believers away from You, Father. Give me
the strength to stay away from their ideas
and turn my thoughts to You. Amen.

Night 162
MORE HOPE WITH JESUS

"If the base of the building is destroyed, what can
those who are right with God do?" The Lord is in
His holy house. The Lord's throne is in heaven.
His eyes see as He tests the sons of men.

PSALM 11:3–4

Jesus said, "In the world you will have much trouble.
But take hope! I have power over the world!" (John 16:33).
Some trouble is outside our control. We can't stop earthquakes, tsunamis, or hurricanes. Some trouble we bring on
ourselves through greed, jealousy, anger, and disobedience.
We may never understand why God allows His people to
suffer. But we do know that regardless of the way things
appear, our loving God is still in control of our world and our
lives. As Christians, we can help those in need. We can rebuild cities hit by natural disasters. And, even more important, we can help rebuild lives by telling people about Jesus!

Heavenly Father, I am always increasing my trust
in You. When bad things happen, it is enough
to know that You are in control. Amen.

Night 163
GOD HIMSELF

"I am the First and the Last.
I am the beginning and the end."
REVELATION 22:13

Is Jesus God? Yes, He is! Jesus is a part of God equal to Him in every way. Our God is unique among the religions of the world. No other religion has a God whose Son is equal to the Father.

The Bible is unique because in it God reveals who He is. Jesus is God come to earth as a man—but not like any human. Jesus is God Himself coming into the world to save us from sin. And God is also the Holy Spirit, the one called the Helper who guides us every day. Our God is one perfect God with three equal parts—Father, Son, and Holy Spirit—now and forever.

Jesus, I learn how to live by Your human example, and I trust in You as my God—Father, Son, and Holy Spirit—three persons, one God, one perfect You! Amen.

Night 164
HE LOVED US FIRST

We love Him because He loved us first.
1 JOHN 4:19

*

Where does love begin? The Bible tells us we love because God loves us first. Our love flows from God's bottomless well of devotion to us. He begins the relationship He wants with us, covering us with His love as He adopts us as His children. The power of God's love within us takes over when human love is running on empty. He plants His love in our hearts so we can share Him with others. Love starts with God. He surrounds us with His love. We live in hope and draw from His strength, all because He first loved us.

. . . .

God, the human love I know on earth cannot compare with Your love. When I feel empty, Your love fills me up. Your love is perfect. It never fails. Amen.

Night 165
OBEYING MOM AND DAD

Children, as Christians, obey your parents. This is the right thing to do. Respect your father and mother.
EPHESIANS 6:1–2

✳

Do you always obey your mom and dad? Everyone has bad days when they just want to dig in their heels and say no. That's not what God wants, though. The Bible clearly says that children should obey their parents. And along with obedience, God uses the word *respect*. He wants you to respect your parents as well. Respect means believing that your parents know best and will guide you with their wisdom. In what ways can you show respect both to your parents—and to God?

Father, please forgive me for the times when I disobey my parents and You. Help me to respect you both and to abide by Your words. Amen.

Night 166
JESUS LOVES EVERYONE

A woman came from the land of Canaan. She cried out
to Jesus and said, "Take pity on me, Lord, Son of David!
My daughter has a demon and is much troubled."

MATTHEW 15:22

One day Jesus met a non-Jewish lady who cried out to Him,
"Lord, Son of David"—a common name for the Messiah—and
begged Jesus to heal her little daughter. Jesus at first ignored
her, and finally told her that He was "sent only to the lost
sheep of Israel [the Jews]" (Matthew 15:24 NIV). Why would
Jesus, who loved and accepted everyone, answer her this
way? Because His first priority was to carry His message of
forgiveness of sin to the Israelites, God's people—and *then*
to the rest of the world. Jesus wasn't being mean. He was
just telling her the truth. And afterward, Jesus healed her
daughter, just as she asked. Jesus loves us all.

Dear Jesus, thank You for loving us no matter where
we come from, who we are, or where we live. Amen.

Night 167
BEFORE YOU ASK

*"As soon as you began to pray, an answer
was given, which I have come to tell you.
For you are loved very much."*

DANIEL 9:23

In the middle of praying one day, Daniel's prayer was interrupted by the appearance of the angel Gabriel. "Daniel," he said, "I have now come to give you wisdom and understanding. As soon as you began to pray, an answer was given" (vv. 22–23). Imagine that. As soon as Daniel began to pray, even before he asked God for what he wanted, God had already sent the answer! As He did for Daniel, God knows our needs even before we ask Him. Even before the words leave our lips, God has already heard them, and He has already answered them.

. . . .

Thank You, Lord, for answering my prayers.
Before I ask, You already have the answer.
How great You are, God! Amen.

Night 168
TRUST JESUS TO FORGIVE

Peter remembered the words Jesus had said
to him, "Before a rooster crows, you will
say three times you do not know Me." Peter
went outside and cried with loud cries.

MATTHEW 26:74–75

Peter denied he ever knew Jesus, not once but three times.
Yet Peter went on to do great things. How is that possible?
Peter owned up to his shame. He trusted Jesus to forgive him
and was given great responsibility after Jesus rose from the
dead. When you mess up and take control over something
you shouldn't, be like Peter and trust Jesus to forgive you.
Then serve Him with a thankful heart.

I forget sometimes and try to control things.
Forgive me, Father. Remind me that You
are in control. My life and everyone else's
are in Your capable hands. Amen.

Night 169
GOD IS THERE

Then Job stood up and tore his clothing
and cut the hair from his head. And he
fell to the ground and worshiped.

JOB 1:20

How did Job express sadness when God allowed everything
he owned to be taken away? He followed the traditional
ways of mourning in his culture by tearing his clothes and
shaving his head. But Job also worshipped. Even with the
terrible situation he was in, Job turned to God. Job opened
his heart to the only one who fully understood and could
help him in his time of deepest need. We can learn from Job
that when everything in life seems lost or out of reach, God
is waiting. God understands our sadness and stays with us.

Sadness is a powerful emotion, Lord, but not nearly as
powerful as Your love. I thank You for understanding,
for comforting me, and for sharing my pain. Amen.

UNDERSTANDING GOD'S WORD

But the person who is not a Christian does not understand these words from the Holy Spirit. . . . He cannot understand them because he does not have the Holy Spirit to help him understand.

1 CORINTHIANS 2:14

✳

Paul divides humans into two classes: the unbelievers and the born-again believers—ones who give God total control of their life. Unbelievers may be smart but fail to understand God's Word because worldly wants fill their hearts. Since they don't believe, the Bible's basic truths are hidden from them. On the other hand, born-again believers focus on the thoughts and will of God. His Spirit lives in their hearts and leads, guides, comforts, and speaks to them. The moment we ask forgiveness for our sins and accept Jesus as our Savior, we become God's own. And from then on, we begin to understand His Word.

• •

Heavenly Father, I know people whose hearts are closed to Your Word. Please open their hearts to be born again, to understand, and to trust in You. Amen.

BIRTHRIGHT

Then Jacob gave Esau bread and vegetables,
and Esau ate and drank. Then Esau stood up and
went on his way. So Esau hated his birth-right.

GENESIS 25:34

In Old Testament times, the oldest son was promised a birthright. This meant when his father died, the son inherited all the father had. This was good news for Esau as the oldest son.

One day Esau came home hungry. His brother, Jacob, had a pot of stew simmering on the stove. Esau grabbed for a bowl. Jacob shook his head. "First, sell me your birthright" (Genesis 25:31).

Esau sold his birthright to Jacob for stew and bread. God's Word says, "None of you should. . .forget God like Esau did. . . . For one plate of food he sold this right to his brother" (Hebrews 12:16). Sometimes it's easy for us to trade our God-given treasures for temporary comfort and pleasure.

You are all the things I need, Lord, always and
forever. Help me to remember. Amen.

Night 172
WHAT DO YOU BELIEVE?

"There is no way to be saved from the punishment of sin through anyone else. For there is no other name under heaven given to men by which we can be saved."

ACTS 4:12

✳

Who was Jesus? Believers and nonbelievers think differently. Believers know in their hearts that Jesus is the Son of God. They believe God sent His Son to save us from sin. They understand that when Jesus rose from the dead, it was His guarantee to believers that after their bodies die, their souls will live on, at home with Him in heaven. Most nonbelievers accept that Jesus did exist. But they do not believe that He was the Son of God. They do not believe that after Jesus died on the cross, He came back to life. They don't believe that Jesus can save us from sin; many believe that they don't need saving. What do you believe? Is Jesus your Lord and Savior?

• •

Jesus, You are my Savior and also my Lord. I worship and praise You. I believe that You are the risen Son who came to earth to save me. Thank You, Jesus! Amen.

GOD MAKES IT SO

Samson found a jawbone of a donkey and took
it in his hand. He killed 1,000 men with it.

JUDGES 15:15

✳

Samson was a big man with enormous physical strength. In
the book of Judges, we discover that God allowed Samson
to aggravate and judge the Philistines, who were ruling
harshly over the Israelites. At one point, Samson set their
ields on fire. The Philistines fought back hard against
Samson's family. Samson's own people, afraid of further
violence, arrested Samson and handed him over to the
Philistines. Samson agreed to go with them, but the Spirit
of God came to save him. Samson saw and grabbed a jawbone of a donkey and used it to kill a thousand Philistines!
That never could have happened unless God made it so.

God, You are the one who enables me to
do what seems impossible. All the credit
and praise I give to You. Amen.

Night 174
WHERE IS YOUR TREASURE?

We came into this world with nothing. For sure,
when we die, we will take nothing with us.

1 TIMOTHY 6:7

✴

Some people store up treasures here on earth, and sometimes those treasures become the most important things in their lives. Jesus had something to say about this: "Do not gather together for yourself riches of this earth. . . . Gather together riches in heaven. . . . For wherever your riches are, your heart will be there also" (Matthew 6:19–21). Later, Paul wrote the words in this Bible verse to remind people that when they die, they take nothing with them. That's true when it comes to worldly things, but there are two things that we *can* take with us: our love for God and the promise that we will live forever with Him in heaven.

Father, You are all that really matters.
My treasure is in heaven with You. Amen.

THE GIFT OF A NEW DAY

This is the day that the Lord has made.
Let us be full of joy and be glad in it.

PSALM 118:24

Getting up is easier when you remember the words in Psalm 118:24. God gives us each new day as a gift. He made that day for us, and what we do with it is up to us. You can think of a new day like a blank canvas on which you can paint anything. God wants you to paint a picture full of joy and gladness. How can you do that? By getting up without grumbling, thanking God for a new day, and then going out and spreading around kindness to others. Give it a try tomorrow morning!

I often forget to thank You in the
morning for giving me a brand-new day.
Thank You for all my days, God! Amen.

Night 176
THE PROMISE OF BRIGHTER DAYS

His loving-pity never ends. It is new
every morning. He is so very faithful.
LAMENTATIONS 3:22–23

✴

This Bible passage reminds us that God's love and understanding have no end. He gives us the opportunity to put our bad day in the past and start fresh the next day. Our God is always faithful. That means we can count on Him never to leave us. Even when we get ourselves into a real mess, God hangs in there with us—not to punish us, but to help us! Trust in His love every day. Allow Him to help you turn a not-so-good day into a great one!

Lord, You are my best friend. You help me through my troubles and brighten up my days. Amen.

HOSPITALITY

Do not forget to be kind to strangers and let them stay in your home. Some people have had angels in their homes without knowing it.

HEBREWS 13:2

✳

Hebrews 13:2 is a verse about *hospitality*—showing kindness to strangers. Today, most strangers to whom we extend generosity and hospitality are probably not angels. Still, we can't know if someday God will allow us to entertain an angel without us knowing it. When you practice hospitality, God might be using you to minister to others. But in today's world, you need to be careful with strangers. Talk about this with your parents: What are some safe ways that you can show kindness to someone you don't know?

God, teach me to be wise when being kind to strangers. Teach me new ways to minister to others and show them Your amazing love. Amen.

GOD'S POWER IS YOUR POWER TOO

"Power belongs to you, God,
and with you, Lord, is unfailing love."

PSALM 62:11–12 NIV

✳

Today's verses are from a psalm written by King David. David was aware of God's power and love, and he did his best to honor God with worship and praise. He pleased God, and in return God made him a great king. He called David "a man after my own heart." God said, "He will do everything I want him to do" (Acts 13:22 NIV). God's power belongs to you too! His love for you is greater than any other love. The strength He gives you isn't necessarily muscle strength. Instead, He gives you a spirit strong enough to smash whatever trouble gets in your way.

• •

Father, strength isn't about muscles and
physical power; it's about the power You give
me to conquer all of life's problems. You are
my strength. Without You, I am weak. Amen.

Night 179
GOD'S FINGERPRINTS

[They] are always listening. . . . But they
are never able to understand the truth.

2 TIMOTHY 3:7

✳

The amount of knowledge humankind has learned since
the Bible was written is mind-boggling. Take what you know
about how people lived back then and compare it to now.
Scientific discoveries have helped us to see the world like
never before. And the truth is this: God's fingerprints are
everywhere. Some people reject the ideas that God created the universe and that He allows us to learn new things.
Learning is good, but learning apart from God's will is not.
We need to give God the thanks but also keep our minds
on His rules for what is right and good, and not our own.

Dear Father, I praise You for all the good things
You have allowed us to learn and do. Help us
all to follow Your will as we learn. Amen.

Night 180
FOLLOWING JESUS

Jesus got into the boat. The man who had had the demons asked to go with Him.

MARK 5:18

✳

There was a man filled with demons who cried out to Jesus to help him. Jesus told the demons to come out of the man and to go into a herd of pigs nearby. The demons did what Jesus said. They entered the pigs, and then the pigs ran into the sea and died! Seeing what Jesus had done, the man wanted to go with Jesus and follow Him. But Jesus had something else in mind. Instead, Jesus sent him back to the nonbelievers. Then something wonderful happened. That man told all the people about the incredible thing Jesus had done for him, and all of them were amazed. In that way, the man *did* follow Jesus. He became like a disciple spreading God's Word.

Jesus, sometimes I feel uncomfortable with nonbelievers. Teach me not to be shy about sharing Your Word. Show me what to do and say. Amen.

Night 181
A GOOD FUTURE

"'For I know the plans I have for you,' says
the Lord, 'plans for well-being and not for
trouble, to give you a future and a hope.'"

JEREMIAH 29:11

✳

In Jeremiah 29:11, the prophet's reassuring words of hope
must have been comforting to the Israelites. The same is
true today. When God promises something, He delivers!
Sometimes hope comes in the form of a second chance
when we think we have failed. Or in the words of a doctor
who has a cure for an illness. Hope often comes with a
loving gesture, a warm hug, or an encouraging word. Hope
is one of God's most precious gifts. God wants to forgive
our sins and lead us on to a good future—just as He did for
the Israelites. He has great plans for you. That's His promise!

Father, You provide hope when things seem
hopeless. Trusting in Your plans for me brings
me joy. My future is in Your hands, so how
can it be anything but good? Amen.

Night 182
COMFORTING OTHERS

"All of you bring trouble instead of comfort."

JOB 16:2

Job speaks the words in this verse. He tells his three friends—Bildad, Eliphaz, and Zophar—who had come to comfort him that all they were doing was making him feel worse. Job had lost everything but his wife in a series of "accidents" when Satan tried to break his faith.

When Job's friends arrived, they sat silently with him for a while, but then they began to question why Job had suffered. Finally, they decided that Job must have done some terrible sins to get himself into such a mess. That's when Job told them what bad comforters they were. When our friends are going through hard times, we should do our best to be loving and godly comforters.

Father God, when I am suffering, You know the perfect ways to comfort me. Please teach me to comfort others with true, godly love. Amen.

Night 183
INSPIRED BY GOD

"I say to you now, stay away from these men and leave them alone. If this teaching and work is from men, it will come to nothing. If it is from God, you will not be able to stop it. You may even find yourselves fighting against God."

ACTS 5:38–39

✳

Peter and his friends were arrested and brought before the high court for preaching about Jesus. They were sentenced to die after Peter bravely spoke of Jesus' resurrection. Gamaliel, an important and respected man, gave the advice to set Peter and the others free. He said that if Peter's actions were inspired by man, they would fail. But if inspired by God, nothing would stop them. The judges, realizing they'd lose in any fight against God, released Peter and the others. When we face obstacles while doing God's work, we can carry on, trusting that God's plan will always win.

Dear God, I won't worry when obstacles get in my way. You have a perfect plan for me, and nothing can stop it. Amen.

Night 184
GOD NEVER FORGETS YOU

"See, I have marked your names on My hands."
ISAIAH 49:16

✳

Have you ever had a bad day turn into a bad week. . .turn into a bad month. . .turn into a bad year? The Israelites found themselves in those times. As their sin increased, God was preparing to hold them accountable. They struggled, thinking that maybe God had forgotten or abandoned them. But God would never do that! He said, "See, I have marked your names on My hands." In the middle of troubling times, it's tempting to think that God has forgotten us. But He hasn't! It is His nail-scarred hand that reaches down from heaven and holds our own.

· ·

Jesus, the scars on Your hands are because
of my sin—a reminder of my salvation.
My name is written in heaven as a child of
God. Oh, thank You, Lord Jesus! Amen.

Night 185
OBEYING GOD'S LAWS

"You put away the Laws of God
and obey the laws made by men."

MARK 7:8

Obeying the law is a good thing, something everyone should do. But what about God's laws? Do most people obey them? The Ten Commandments are God's most well-known laws, but there are others. Entire books of the Bible are dedicated to God's laws. It is almost impossible for a person to know all the laws written in the Bible. Although it's impossible to follow every law in the Bible, we can be careful to follow the ones that we do know. We try hard to follow man-made laws, and we should try just as hard—no, even harder!—to follow God's laws.

· ·

Teach me Your laws, Father. Then remind
me to follow them as best I can. Amen.

Night 186
HONORING PARENTS

"Honor your father and your mother,
so your life may be long in the land
the Lord your God gives you."

EXODUS 20:12

Let's see how good you are at remembering your house rules. How many can you list? God says to honor your mom and dad. One way to honor them is by willingly obeying their rules. *Willingly* means being respectful while doing what you are told. If there is a rule that you disagree with, then ask to quietly discuss it. And if your parents still say no, then accept their answer with respect. Someday you may be a parent too. By then, you will have been around a long time and will understand the importance of house rules. In the meantime, follow God's law and honor your parents.

Dear heavenly Father, forgive me for disobeying some of the rules my parents have set for me. Help me to obey and honor my parents with respect. Amen.

Night 187
HONORING GOD

Give great honor to the Lord with me.
PSALM 34:3

You should honor God above all others and in everything you do. Here are some ways to honor Him. Honor God when you play by sharing with your friends. Honor God with your words. Honor God with your thoughts. Honor God with your attitude. Honor God with your friendships. One of the very best ways to honor God is by setting a good example for others in the way you live. Can you think of more ways to honor the Lord? How can you honor Him in your community? At school? At church?

God, teach me ways to honor You. I want You
to be pleased with everything I do. Amen.

Night 188
ACT OF LOVE

Have a true love for each other.
Love covers many sins.

1 PETER 4:8

We should reflect Jesus' true love by forgiving others. Think about this: if you forgive someone for something they've done, your forgiveness can breathe new life into that relationship. If you and your best friend have a fight, you both feel terrible. The only way to fix it is to forgive each other. And when you do forgive, your broken friendship comes back to life again. Your love for each other wins over the sin that broke you up. Memorize tonight's Bible verse so you will have it in your heart whenever you need to forgive. And remember too, Jesus' great act of love.

Dear Jesus, please help me to love
others the way that You do. Amen.

LIVING WATER

"For My people have done two sinful things: They have turned away from Me, the well of living waters. And they have cut out of the rock wells for water for themselves. They are broken wells that cannot hold water."

JEREMIAH 2:13

In Jeremiah 2:13, God uses this example to remind His people to follow Him. The people were all caught up in worldly things, selfishly wanting for themselves. It was as if they had dug a well and filled it up with all this bad stuff. God said that sooner or later that "well" was going to crack, leaving nothing but sin in their lives. Then there would be no way for them to go to heaven. But God reminded them that His "well" would not crack. He called Himself "the well of living waters." God meant if they turned from sin and followed Him, they could live forever with Him in heaven. Ask God now for some of His living water! There's plenty for everyone.

Dear God, fill me up with Your living water. Forgive me for my sins and lead me in all my ways. Amen.

Night 190
GOD KNOWS EVERYTHING

He came to a cave, and stayed there. The word of the Lord came to him, and said, "What are you doing here, Elijah?"

1 KINGS 19:9

In 1 Kings 19:9, God already knew what had brought Elijah to the point of such misery that he prayed to God to take his life. God knew that Elijah was in serious trouble and was running in fear for his life. Despite knowing all this, God still asked Elijah why he was hiding out in a cave.

Sometimes we live in a way that causes God to ask us the question He asked Elijah. God sees and knows everything we do. Listen for His voice inside your heart. He might be asking you to stop and think about what you're doing. Aren't you thankful He cares enough to ask?

Father, You always see me. Help me to stop, think, and act according to Your will. Amen.

Night 191
STRENGTH TO STAND

Jesus was full of the Holy Spirit when He returned from the Jordan River. Then He was led by the Holy Spirit to a desert.

LUKE 4:1

After Jesus was baptized, He went into the desert. He was led there by the Holy Spirit to face Satan. For forty days, God allowed Satan to tempt Jesus to see if His human side might rebel and give in. But He never gave in. He used scripture verses to answer Satan, and after Satan tempted Him in every way, he left Jesus alone. Those forty days, when Jesus might have struggled to remain true to His Father, give hope to the rest of us. Because of that experience, the Lord stands right beside us, understanding us when we face testing times. You can always turn to Jesus, because He knows what it's like—He understands you.

Jesus, You understand what it's like to be human and face worldly temptations. Sometimes it's hard to resist! Please give me strength to stand up to Satan. Amen.

Night 192

GOD'S PERFECT PLAN FOR YOU

Your eyes saw me before I was put together.
And all the days of my life were written in
Your book before any of them came to be.

PSALM 139:16

God has a special plan for everyone. The Bible talks about several people God set apart for greatness: Moses, who led the Israelites out of Egypt; David, Israel's great king; John the Baptist, called to prepare the way of the Lord. But God also knows the days of ordinary people. Every day He is moving you forward in His plan for you. King David wrote, "All You know is too great for me. It is too much for me to understand" (Psalm 139:6). Although you might not understand the path God has planned for you, you can be sure that the plan is perfectly in line with His will.

God, how can You know all about everyone who has or ever will live? Your ways are so far beyond my understanding, and yet You love me. You are so wonderful! Amen.

Night 193
GOD IS LIKE A FIRE

For our God is a fire that destroys everything.
HEBREWS 12:29

✳

This verse compares God to fire. A fire can destroy every-thing. After a fierce forest fire, there appears to be nothing left. But watch, and soon you will see signs of rebirth appear with shoots of green growth and the return of life. What was destroyed comes back to life—a comparison to Jesus' body and His resurrection! When we trust God, we allow Him to burn away our selfishness, our pride, and anything that blocks His light from shining through our lives. His love burns away our sinfulness and gives us a fresh new start.

Lord, cleanse me of my sin. Burn away my old ways.
Create in me a new and more holy life. Amen.

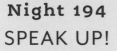

Night 194
SPEAK UP!

Then He began to say to them, "The Holy Writings
you have just heard have been completed today."

LUKE 4:21

Jesus declared Himself the Son of God in front of a home-town audience. As Christians, we often are among non-believers (perhaps in school, at sporting events, and even in our neighborhoods). It's difficult to stand up in front of people who know you and say, "I am a child of God." Some will think you've gone crazy; others will poke fun. Is it worth the hassle? Wouldn't it be easier to stay quiet? But that isn't what it's all about. Jesus spoke up—and God wants us to do the same. Face others and tell them who you are. It won't be easy, but God will provide the courage you need.

. . . .

Dear God, take away any shyness I have about
sharing You with my family and friends. You are my
Father, and I am proud to let others know. Amen.

Night 195
GOD NEVER SLEEPS

He will not let your feet go out from under you.
He Who watches over you will not sleep.

PSALM 121:3

✳

Today's Bible verse tells us that God does not sleep. He watches over us, never once taking His eyes off us even for a few quick moments of rest. God guards us all the time, 24-7. The Lord stays up all night, looking after us as we sleep. He patiently keeps His eyes on us even when we sleep away from home. He always comforts us when fear or illness makes us toss and turn at night. Like when your mom or dad tiptoes into your room to check on you while you sleep, God surrounds you even when you don't realize it. You can sleep well every night because God is watching over you.

God, how thankful I am that You never sleep.
When I'm asleep, You guard me because I'm
Your child. I love You, Father! Amen.

"For sure, I tell you, unless a seed falls into
the ground and dies, it will only be a seed.
If it dies, it will give much grain."

JOHN 12:24

When planted, a wheat seed's waterproof coating breaks down. Soon, roots emerge and tiny shoots jet upward. Before long, the seed blossoms into a towering stalk filled with countless grains of wheat. In one of His parables, Jesus compared Himself to a wheat seed to emphasize the necessity of His death, the power of His resurrection, and the idea that many souls would be saved because of Him. When you put your faith and trust in Him, your love for Him grows. It's no longer hidden deep inside. Others see your love for Him too. And every time you share Jesus with others, your actions and words might plant His seed in their hearts too!

Jesus, I want Your love to grow within
me. Help others to see it grow and to
want You in their hearts too. Amen.

STAYING TRUE

"But the one who stays true
to the end will be saved."

MATTHEW 24:13

✳

"Staying true" means hanging on to your faith. In good times, it's easy to have faith in God. But when times get hard, we need to be careful that our faith doesn't slip away. It's in those times that God will grow our faith even stronger if we stay true to Him. God makes an important promise at the end of this Bible verse: "But the one who stays true to the end *will be saved.*" Hang tight to your faith in Him. Stay true. And when bad times come, remember God's promise—He will save you.

Dear God, I know I can count on You to save me
from trouble. Help me, please, to stay strong
in my faith and true to You always. Amen.

Night 198
WRONG PATHS

Then the angel of the Lord went farther.
He stood in a narrow place where there
was no way to turn to the right or the left.

NUMBERS 22:26

Sometimes in life we head in the wrong direction. We start walking down a path that God knows will get us into trouble. That's when God might start putting obstacles in our way. It's Him saying, "Stop. Think about where you're going. Is it the right direction?" When your plans don't seem to be working out, stop and pray. Ask God to show you whether you should keep going or go a different way.

God, if I head down the wrong path in life,
make me stop. I want to follow the way
that You have set for me. Amen.

Night 199
ONLY BECAUSE OF GOD

*If anyone thinks he is important when
he is nothing, he is fooling himself.*

GALATIANS 6:3

A grandfather asked his grandson, "What do you think you want to do when you grow up?"

"I *know* what I want to do," the boy said. "I'm going to be president!"

"And how important are you right now?" the grandfather asked. His question took the boy by surprise.

He thought and then answered, "I don't know. I'm just a kid." In God's eyes, the boy was just as important at that moment as he would be if he were president. No matter how important we think we are, what matters to God is just that we understand we are nothing without Him. Every good thing we accomplish is because of Him.

- -

Heavenly Father, You have blessed me with accomplishments here on earth—but what I have achieved is nothing without You. All the glory and honor belong to You. Amen.

Night 200
PROOF IN JESUS

*Every word of God has been proven true. He is
a safe-covering to those who trust in Him.*

PROVERBS 30:5

✳

The Bible is ancient. We know that because some of those
ancient Bibles have been discovered, and the words in
those Bibles say the same things. Archaeologists have
discovered so much that proves the existence of people,
places, and things in the Bible. Maps and names and mes-
sages carved into stone were found that support what's
in the Bible. But what's important isn't the physical proof
that the Bible is 100 percent true—it's that God requires
His people to trust in Him. He wants us to have so much
trust in Him that we believe—*without proof*—that He exists
and that His words are true. Do you trust God enough to
believe that the Bible is perfectly true?

I believe the Bible as truth, Lord. I need no evidence.
My proof is in You, the one who cannot lie. Amen.

Night 201

PUTTING YOUR BLESSINGS TO WORK

It is bad for those who are taking it easy in Zion, and for those who feel safe on the mountain of Samaria, you great men of the most important nation, to whom the people of Israel come!

AMOS 6:1

Amos was a shepherd who also grew sycamore figs. He was a poor man. But God called him to be a prophet and carry His words to the rich leaders of Israel (Amos 7:14–15). God was disgusted with these leaders, and He wanted them to know it! Amos went to Zion, where the rich men lived, and gave them God's message: "It is bad that you great men of God's most important nation are taking it easy." In other words, "Wake up! Get with it! God gave you these blessings. Now put them to work for Him!" Remember Amos' words. When God blesses you, don't just be satisfied and take it easy. Get busy and put those blessings to work!

Lord, it means everything when You are satisfied with me. Wake me up! Send me out to work for You. Amen.

Night 202
TOO GOOD TO BE TRUE

Lot looked and saw that the Jordan valley was well watered everywhere like the garden of the Lord.

GENESIS 13:10

The pastureland wasn't big enough for the livestock that belonged to Abram and his nephew, so Abram offered Lot first choice of the surrounding areas. Wanting the best land, Lot moved onto the plains of the Jordan Valley. But Lot discovered that the people who lived there were sinning against God. When their evil ways grew to the point of no return, God destroyed the place with fire and brimstone. Only Lot and his two daughters escaped. Lot took what looked like the best but ended up losing everything except what he and his daughters could carry. Sometimes there's wisdom in holding back and wondering, *Is it too good to be true?*

God, help me to carefully weigh what looks
too good to be true. Before I make a decision,
remind me to hold back and seek Your will. Amen.

Night 203
SEEING JESUS

*Then He turned to His followers and said
without anyone else hearing, "Happy
are those who see what you see!"*

LUKE 10:23

Jesus' disciples were blessed men. Why? Because they were able to see Jesus in the flesh, to live, talk, eat, and walk with Him as a human being. And they paid dearly for the privilege. Many people hated them for loving the Lord. Jesus' earthly mission wasn't finished when His body died. He would appear again to the disciples and guide them as they spread the gospel in foreign lands, and He had also taught them to look for Him in "the least of these." This means that we still get to see Jesus! Until we join Him in heaven, we will see the Lord at work in others as they help the humble, the hungry, the lonely, and the poor.

Jesus, allow me to see You through the world's people. Open my eyes to Your gentle compassion, the truths of Your teaching, Your amazing forgiveness, and Your deepest love. Amen.

Night 204
GOD WORKS EVERYTHING OUT

"Look among the nations, and see! Be surprised and full of wonder! For I am doing something in your days that you would not believe if you were told."

HABAKKUK 1:5

✳

"O Lord. . . I cry out to You, 'We are being hurt!' . . . Why do you make me see sins and wrong-doing? . . . For the sinful are all around those who are right and good, so what is right looks like sin" (Habakkuk 1:2–4). The prophet Habakkuk said those words about 2,600 years ago, but if you think about it, we live in a world with similar problems today. Habakkuk had to trust that God was in control, and He would work everything out for the good of His people (Romans 8:28). God is just as much in control today. He has a good plan for those who love Him. We might not understand why bad things happen in the world. But God sees, and He understands.

God, I worry that nothing seems to be going right, but then I remember—You are in control, working it all out for good. Amen.

Night 205
NEVER HIDE YOUR FAITH

The Lord turned and looked at Peter. He remembered
the Lord had said, "Before a rooster crows, you
will say three times that you do not know Me."

LUKE 22:61

Jesus had just been arrested, and Peter, afraid for his own life,
lied and said he didn't know Jesus. In Jesus' time of greatest
need, He turned to Peter—His friend—and heard him lie,
heard him put his own safety before Jesus'. The expression
on Jesus' face made Peter run away. Some Christians today
are like Peter. They are afraid to say that they know and love
Jesus, afraid that others might make fun of them. . .or worse.
So they blend in with the crowd and keep quiet about their
faith. Imagine the expression on Jesus' face as He sees you
pretending that you don't know Him. He loves you! Don't
disappoint Him by covering up your faith.

Dear Jesus, forgive me when I don't share You
with nonbelievers who I think will make fun
of me. Give me courage to stand up and say
that I'm proud to call You my Lord! Amen.

Night 206
A CALL TO ACTION

Whatever your hand finds to do,
do it with all your strength.

ECCLESIASTES 9:10

✳

Tonight's Bible verse is a call to action. It tells us to put all our effort and strength into everything we do. Whatever you do, think of it as something you are doing for God. Your best effort should go into staying away from what you know is wrong. But if you do mess up, ask God to forgive you. Depend on His wisdom to give you strength not to make the same mistake again. When you give, give your best; when you work, do your best work; when you pray, pray with all your heart. And when you've done the best you can, leave the rest up to God.

Lord, please keep the thought fresh in my mind that whatever I do, I am doing it for You. Then help me to do my best. Amen.

SHINE THE LOVE OF JESUS

Some are weak. I have become weak so I might lead them to Christ. I have become like every person so in every way I might lead some to Christ.

1 CORINTHIANS 9:22

Jesus is for everyone. There is plenty of room in the kingdom of heaven for every person ever born. Jesus went out of His way to reach people wherever they were. He did everything that could have been done to offer hope. Jesus knew how to reach people! How amazing is it to think that God's Son was able to relate to all people on a level that no one else in history ever could? You can help lead others to Jesus! Show kindness and be at peace with everyone so they can see the love of Jesus shine through you.

O Jesus, let Your perfect love shine
through me, especially in hard times
and in difficult situations. Amen.

Night 208
GOD'S UNFAILING LOVE

Show Your great loving-kindness. You save
by Your right hand the people that come to
You for help from those who hate them.

PSALM 17:7

David certainly wasn't feeling loved when he wrote the words in this scripture verse—he was on the run! His prayer in this verse is for forgiveness and protection. While running from his enemies, David called out to his God of unfailing love. Giving in to misery and frustration must have been tempting, but instead David kept his focus on God in the middle of a dangerous situation. This week, look for the ways God shows His love for you. It may be in a sunrise that takes your breath away, in something fun that you hadn't planned for, or in an unexpected compliment from a friend. God's unfailing love is at work in your life in wonderful ways.

Father God, remind me of all the little ways that You
love me. You are so good to me. I love You too! Amen.

Night 209
SWEET LIKE HONEY

Pleasing words are like honey. They are sweet
to the soul and healing to the bones.

PROVERBS 16:24

This Bible verse compares kind words to honey. Honey is
a symbol of happiness and health in the Bible. It is a good
food. The Bible says that John the Baptist ate lots of honey.
It's basically all that he ate! We often forget that the power
of our words can make someone feel good or cut deep into
the heart and cause pain. Choose your words carefully—coat
them with honey. Pass on an overheard compliment, say
"I love you," or write a note of appreciation to share God's
love through your words.

Lord, from now on, I will think before I
speak and choose my words wisely. Amen.

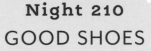

Night 210
GOOD SHOES

Wear shoes on your feet which
are the Good News of peace.

EPHESIANS 6:15

Good footwear was important in Bible times. People often walked wherever they needed to go, sometimes walking for many miles wearing leather sandals on their feet. Paul might have been thinking of Jesus and His disciples walking from city to town preaching God's Word. Or, he might have been thinking of the sandals worn by Roman soldiers— sandals with spikes that sunk into the ground and allowed them to stand firm in battles. Whatever Paul had in mind for shoes, his message is clear: wherever you go, go peacefully and spread the good news about Jesus. Tell others that Jesus came to save them from sin and make a place for them in heaven.

God, I want my feet to help me carry the good news and to always be ready to defend it. Amen.

PURE, GOOD, AND READY

Take away the waste from the silver, and a
silver pot comes out for the workman.

PROVERBS 25:4

Silver is rarely found in the earth in a pure state. Usually,
when silver is dug out of the rocks, it's mixed with the sul-
phide ore of lead or other less valuable minerals. It then
must be put through a refining process to remove the waste.
The Bible describes God's people as silver and the Lord as
a "purifier of silver" who puts them through the refiner's
fire to remove the impurities (Malachi 3:2–3 NIV). In other
words, God is always working on us to remove the bad and
useless stuff from our hearts. His goal is to make us pure,
good, and ready for heaven. Jesus is the one who removes
the sin from our lives. Because of Him, we are like the best
silver—fit for God, our King.

Jesus, please work on me. Make me pure
for God, like the finest silver. Amen.

Night 212
GENEROUS FORGIVENESS

Then Jesus said, "Father, forgive them. They
do not know what they are doing." And they
divided His clothes by drawing names.

LUKE 23:34

No human will ever be as forgiving as Jesus. That's a fact.
But God wants us to try. Take a few minutes to think about
the people who've hurt you or those you don't trust.
Are they any worse than the soldiers who killed Jesus? Do
you think Jesus would forgive them if He were in your place?
Forgiveness is one of the biggest tests we face in life—and
one of the blessings we need the most. Jesus died so we
would be forgiven for every sin we ever do. Let's try to be
like Him as much as we can and be forgiving toward others.

Father, help me to forgive those who have hurt me—
the way You have so generously forgiven me. Amen.

Night 213
HOLD GOD'S HAND

"For I am the Lord your God Who holds
your right hand, and Who says to you,
'Do not be afraid. I will help you.'"

ISAIAH 41:13

Hundreds of Bible verses touch on things like our emotions of fear, anxiety, and worry. Fear is nothing new. People have been afraid of one thing or another since the beginning of time. Maybe that's why, in verse after verse, God reminds us of His presence and offers us peace, as He did for countless others. Reread tonight's verse. God is so loving toward us with His words. He holds our hand and says four important words: "I will help you." It's His invitation to hold on to His hand and accept His help. When you feel afraid, take God's hand!

Take my hand, Lord, and help me. Your strong,
gentle touch will take away my fear. Amen.

Night 214
DON'T LET PRIDE GET IN THE WAY

A day was set aside. On that day Herod put on purple clothes a king wears. He sat on his throne and spoke to the people. They all started to speak with a loud voice, "This is the voice of a god, not of a man."

ACTS 12:21–22

King Herod understood God's rules, but pride got in the way. He put his own need to be kingly above God's commands—and that got him into trouble. Herod set up a festival of games to be played in the kingdom's stadium. He put on his kingly purple robes, sat on his throne, and spoke to his people. The crowd began to worship Herod, and he accepted their claim that he was a god. According to the Jewish historian Josephus, God's angel infected Herod with parasites, and he became very sick. Herod's story is a good reminder not to let pride or anything else get in the way of doing your best to follow God's rules.

Lord, please forgive me for those times when I've done what I know is wrong. Amen.

Night 215
A PURE HEART

*Keep your heart pure for out of it
are the important things of life.*

PROVERBS 4:23

＊

When was the last time your heart got a checkup? When you went for your checkup, the doctor probably used a stethoscope to listen to your heart. But there is another kind of heart checkup, one better than any doctor can perform. God wants you to do a check of your own heart. What's in there? Whatever is in your heart will come out in how you behave. When your heart is pure, only good things will come out of it. When sin creeps in, your words and actions will reflect that too. How have you been behaving lately? Is there some sin in your heart that you need to get rid of? Tell Jesus all about it and ask Him to give you a pure heart that's pleasing to God.

· ·

Lord Jesus, I've checked my heart and there's
sin in there. I want it gone. Please forgive
me for my bad behavior and help me to
have a good and pure heart. Amen.

Night 216
PROMISE KEEPER

When Jesus had said this, He showed
them His hands and feet.

LUKE 24:40

Think about Jesus. He could have called thousands of angels to save Him from the cross, but instead He suffered an awful death. He came to keep a promise—Jesus, the Son of God, came to earth to save us from sin and lead us to heaven. He was the promise that God would never abandon us. He loved us in spite of our sin. When Jesus rose from the dead, He showed His followers the nail marks in His hands and feet. His torn flesh spoke without words: *Do you see how much I love you?* Jesus kept His promise to us. Let's do our best to honor Him in such a way that when we get to heaven, God will say, "I saw how much you loved Me."

Jesus, You were true to Your word.
You never backed out. You always did what
You promised. Help me to show my love
for You by keeping my promises too. Amen.

Night 217
ROCKY PATHS

A voice is calling, "Make the way ready
for the Lord in the desert. Make the road
in the desert straight for our God."

ISAIAH 40:3

An ancient custom in Bible times required that a representative be sent ahead of an important person to prepare the road. He removed obstacles like rocks and boulders and filled in the potholes. Travel was easier when the crooked road became straight and even. Our journey in life sometimes leads us down rocky paths. We need someone to lead the way to get us out of trouble. We want to do what is right, but we stumble. God prepares our way for us. If we rely on Him as our representative, He will remove all the obstacles that get in our way. He makes the crooked road straight and gives us strength to keep walking.

Dear God, You go on ahead of me,
clearing the obstacles and lighting
my way. Thank You, Father! Amen.

Night 218
DON'T WORRY!

Do not worry. Learn to pray about everything.
Give thanks to God as you ask Him for what you need.

PHILIPPIANS 4:6

"Do not worry" sounds like great advice, but most of us have the feeling that it only works for some people but not for us. We worry about today's troubles, like moving to a new place, taking a test in school, and whether we will play well in Saturday's game to help our team win. The key to not worrying is taking our problems to God in prayer, thanking Him for solving past problems, and trusting Him to work out the new ones. When we do that, we can stop worrying. We've handed our problem over to God, and we can follow where He leads us.

Father, worrying makes me tired. I ask You to take all my problems and work them out for my good. Show me the way, Lord, and I will follow You. Amen.

Night 219
NOT EVEN DARKNESS

The Light shines in the darkness. The darkness
has never been able to put out the Light.

JOHN 1:5

✳

If you look at the sky on a clear night, you will see the moon
and stars. But what about on a dark, cloudy night? Has God
taken away the stars and the moon? No! They are still there
but hidden from our sight. It's like that with Jesus sometimes.
He says, "I am the Light of the world" (John 8:12). But a dark
cloud of sin can keep us from seeing Jesus at work in our
lives. Beyond that cloud, He is still there—as mighty, powerful,
and loving as ever. We can't keep clouds from preventing
us from seeing the stars, but we can remove that cloud of
sin from our lives in order to see Jesus. He's there waiting
for us. Nothing, not even the darkness, can keep Him away.

Jesus, please remove anything that keeps me from
following You and seeing Your work in my life. Amen.

Night 220
NEVER LONELY

God makes a home for those who are alone.
He leads men out of prison into happiness
and well-being. But those who fight
against Him live in an empty desert.

PSALM 68:6

God understands what it's like to be lonely. That's why He
has put people around you who love you! And who loves
you more than anyone on earth? God does! His love for
you is perfect and forever. Whatever causes loneliness, God
doesn't want it! He promises to never leave us alone. He
wants to lift us up, dry our tears, and make us feel happy
and safe. God has a way of bringing people into our lives
exactly when we need them. If you feel alone, don't keep
it to yourself. Reach out to someone—a family member,
teacher, or friend. Then trust God with the rest.

Thank You, God, for the people who love me. Thank You
too for Your perfect love. Whenever I feel alone, bring
people into my life to help me. In Jesus' name, amen.

STRENGTH TO KEEP GOING

Joseph went to have his and Mary's names
written in the books of the nation. Mary was his
promised wife and soon to become a mother.

LUKE 2:5

Caesar Augustus ruled that a count of all the people be taken,
so everyone went to their hometown to register. Joseph
and Mary traveled from Nazareth to Bethlehem, where she
gave birth to Jesus (Luke 2:1–7). The journey from Nazareth
to Bethlehem was almost a hundred miles—through rugged
land, up and down steep hills. The trip would take a minimum of five days on foot, and at night Joseph and Mary
would need safe places to camp. That Mary made the trip
is a miracle because she was nearly ready to have her baby.
Everyone experiences long, tough journeys in life. And God
understands! When we're tired, He gives us strength to keep
on going.

Lord, life's journey is sometimes like climbing up a
steep hill. I know that You understand. Take my hand
and walk with me. Give me strength to go on. Amen.

Night 222
SEEKING GOD AND GROWING FAITH

*Even if an army gathers against me,
my heart will not be afraid.*

PSALM 27:3

In Psalm 27, David was thinking about what might happen to him. There were people who hated him and had tried to kill him. Yet, as David wrote this psalm, he recognized God's presence and power at work in his life. David promised that no matter what, he would trust God—because he knew it was safe and wise to do so. Overconfidence can be a problem, but godly confidence is important to have in our lives. Without it, our faith begins to fail. Trusting God completely is an expression of faith and the most important step to winning when Satan tries to put obstacles in our way. The more we seek God, the more our faith grows! David is proof of that.

Father God, my faith grows stronger as I learn
to trust You not only with big things but also
with the small things in my life. Amen.

Night 223
GOD IS ON YOUR SIDE

You have never been tempted to sin in any different
way than other people. God is faithful. He will
not allow you to be tempted more than you can
take. But when you are tempted, He will make
a way for you to keep from falling into sin.

1 CORINTHIANS 10:13

Is there something you know you shouldn't do, but it's hard
to keep from doing it? Satan is the one who tries to get
you to sin. You might think that he is tempting you more
than he tempts others. But tonight's verse says that there
is nothing unusual about what tempts you. Satan works
very hard on Christians. But we know from 1 Corinthians
10:13 that God steps in to help us. No matter how weak
we may feel, with God on our side we can walk away from
anything Satan wants us to do. Isn't it great to know that
God is here for us?

Lord, it's hard to keep from sinning sometimes.
Please help me to be strong and do what is right. Amen.

Night 224
REST, LISTEN, AND WAIT

But they who wait upon the Lord will get new strength. They will rise up with wings like eagles. They will run and not get tired. They will walk and not become weak.

ISAIAH 40:31

✳

Imagine this: You are hopelessly lost in the mountains. For days you have been wandering rocky paths, eating whatever berries you can find and looking for a way out. Finally, you are too tired to go on. So, you sit down quietly and wait to be rescued. And then—the shadow of a great winged creature (an eagle!) comes into view. It swoops down, picks you up with its talons, and carries you home! God says that when you feel lost, tired, and weak, you should stop! Rest, listen for His voice, and wait for Him to rescue you. When you put all your faith and trust in Him, He will arrive at just the right time and bless you with the strength you need to go on.

Dear God, I quietly wait for You. Remove all distractions that might keep me from hearing Your voice. Speak to me, Father. I'm listening. Amen.

Night 225
KNOW IN YOUR HEART

"We believe and know You are the Christ.
You are the Son of the Living God."

JOHN 6:69

Many of Jesus' followers found His teachings too difficult to understand, and so they quit following Him. So, Jesus asked His disciples where they stood. Would they leave Him too? Peter answered, "We believe and know You are the Christ. You are the Son of the Living God." The disciples did not just *believe* that Jesus was the Son of God. They *knew* it! They knew in their hearts that Jesus was who He claimed to be. Simply saying that you believe in Jesus isn't enough. You need to know in your heart that He is real and alive today. His Spirit is with you all the time, helping you, leading you, and loving you. Where do you stand? Do you know who Jesus is?

Lord, teach me to know that You are God—real in every way, my Creator, my Savior, and my hope. Amen.

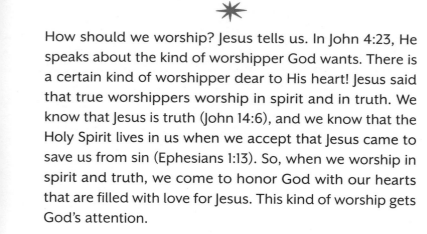

Night 226
IN SPIRIT AND TRUTH

"The time is coming, yes, it is here now, when the true worshipers will worship the Father in spirit and in truth. The Father wants that kind of worshipers."

JOHN 4:23

How should we worship? Jesus tells us. In John 4:23, He speaks about the kind of worshipper God wants. There is a certain kind of worshipper dear to His heart! Jesus said that true worshippers worship in spirit and in truth. We know that Jesus is truth (John 14:6), and we know that the Holy Spirit lives in us when we accept that Jesus came to save us from sin (Ephesians 1:13). So, when we worship in spirit and truth, we come to honor God with our hearts that are filled with love for Jesus. This kind of worship gets God's attention.

O God, when I worship You, send the Holy Spirit to lead me in worshipping You in truth. Amen.

COMFORT IN YOUR SADNESS

*"You are sad now. I will see you again
and then your hearts will be full of joy.
No one can take your joy from you."*

JOHN 16:22

Life on earth isn't always happy. Some days, we cry. And that will continue all our days until we get to heaven. That's when we get to sing and dance and be happy forever! Jesus makes this promise: "I will see you again, and your heart shall rejoice." Until then, if you feel a bit down, don't allow the words of others to beat you up. Remember this: Jesus cried too. He cried when He saw how sad Mary and Martha were when their brother, Lazarus, died (John 11:35). If Jesus, the Son of God, cried, then surely it is okay for you to cry too.

Lord, it is part of being human to cry. But I'm glad that You understand sadness and comfort me. Amen.

Night 228
YOUR HOPES AND DREAMS

For You are my hope, O Lord God.
You are my trust since I was young.

PSALM 71:5

One of the best things you can do right now is to give all your hopes and dreams to God. When you start giving your hopes and dreams to Him at a young age, then it becomes a habit for your lifetime. Trust is a part of giving your hopes and dreams to God. Maybe He has something different and better waiting for you. When you give your hopes and dreams to Him, you also trust Him to give you what is best according to His plan for your life. Spend time every day telling God about your hopes and dreams. Then, someday, many years from now, you can say to Him, "You are my hope, O Lord God. You are my trust since I was young."

Father, I trust You with my hopes and
dreams for now and the future. Amen.

EXCITING PLANS FOR YOU!

"David was a good leader for the people of his day.
He did what God wanted. Then he died and was
put into a grave close to his father's grave."

ACTS 13:36

David began life as the baby brother to his siblings. None of them could have known God's amazing plan for David. God gave him a natural talent for music and poetry, which he used to write many of the Bible's psalms. His God-given leadership abilities gave David success on the battlefield and later as king of Israel. David desired to obey God but failed miserably at times. Yet God looked deep into David's soul and said, "David. . .will please My heart. He will do all I want done" (Acts 13:22). Despite the ups and downs, David accomplished God's plan for his life. God has a good plan for you too. Isn't that exciting?

Thank You for the talents and abilities You
have given me, Lord. I know they are part of
Your plan for me. Help me to use them wisely
and according to Your purpose. Amen.

Night 230
DIVING IN

Then the follower whom Jesus loved said to
Peter, "It is the Lord!" When Peter heard it was
the Lord, he put on his fisherman's coat. (He had
taken it off.) Then he jumped into the water.

JOHN 21:7

"When Peter heard". . .in other words, he hadn't actually
recognized Jesus at that point. But when Peter understood it
was Jesus, risen from the dead, standing there on the shore,
he couldn't get off his fishing boat and to shore fast enough!
He grabbed his coat before jumping into the water. Why?
Because Peter was all about getting to his Lord! After the
resurrection, the disciples never knew when or where they
might meet Jesus. If Jesus came back right now, would you
ask for all kinds of proof and look around to see who is
watching? Or would you follow Peter's example and "dive
in headfirst" to meet Him?

Jesus, call to me, "Here I am," and I will come to You.
I come in faith, wanting to be near You, wanting
to learn all that You have to teach me. Amen.

BE AVAILABLE TO GOD

Then the Lord said to him, "Who has made
man's mouth? Who makes a man not able
to speak or hear? Who makes one blind
or able to see? Is it not I, the Lord?"

EXODUS 4:11

✳

Throughout Exodus chapter 4, we repeatedly hear Moses tell
God why God's plan won't work, finally stating, "Uh, Lord,
You've picked the wrong guy for the job. . .I'm not good
enough." When God asks us to do something, we sometimes have a similar response. In our attempts to tell God
why He's wrong, God's response would surely be something
like, "I know you better than you know you, so get on with
it. . . . Oh, and don't forget. This isn't a solo mission" (see
Exodus 4:12). Often, what we label "impossible" and "imperfect" is God's perfect way to execute His plans. It's up to us
to make ourselves available, remembering we're not alone.

Father, I know that the impossible is possible
when You and I tackle it together. I'm ready.
I'm willing. Let's go! Amen.

JESUS IS ALL YOU NEED

It is so much better to know Christ Jesus my Lord.
I have lost everything for Him. And I think of
these things as worth nothing so that I can have
Christ. I want to be as one with Him. I could not
be right with God by what the Law said I must do.
I was made right with God by faith in Christ.

PHILIPPIANS 3:8–9

Paul gave up everything to follow Jesus. He traded a life-time of riches and comfort for Jesus' promise of forever life in heaven. Paul gave up everything willingly. In fact, he thought none of his past stuff and the admiration of others was worth anything anymore. All he wanted was Jesus. And Paul understood that Jesus was all he needed. He wasn't made right with God by following the Jewish laws. Instead, he pleased God through his solid faith in Christ. Think about it: Is your faith in Jesus strong, like Paul's, or do you put more faith in whatever you have right now?

Lord, I am the richest kid on earth because I have You
in my heart and the promise of eternal life. Amen.

FAITH WITHOUT DOUBT

Let no one show little respect for you because you are
young. Show other Christians how to live by your life.

1 TIMOTHY 4:12

✴

Most of the time, age has its privileges. The older you become,
the more responsibilities you are allowed until you're all
grown up and you can do whatever you choose. It doesn't
work that way with faith. Think about how Jesus said we
should come to Him—like little children! As a young believer,
you probably still remember what it's like to believe without
any of Satan's obstacles getting in your way. Hold on to that
memory and keep believing that way! Then do your best to
remind the grown-ups in your life what it is like to have faith
without doubt. You will be doing them a favor!

• •

Dear God, help me to hold on to my "little kid faith,"
that simple kind of faith without doubt. It is in that
purest form of belief that I am nearest to You. Amen.

Night 234
SURPRISING FAITH

Jesus was surprised when He heard this. He turned to
the people following Him and said, "I tell you, I have
not found so much faith even in the Jewish nation."

LUKE 7:9

It's hard to imagine Jesus being surprised. Yet Luke 7:9 says
that's exactly what happened.

A soldier had sent for Jesus to come to his house and
heal his dying servant. Before Jesus could arrive, however,
the soldier sent another message. He told Jesus he wasn't
worthy to have Jesus come to his home and that he believed
Jesus had the power to heal his servant from where He was.
Jesus was surprised by the soldier's faith. He was moved
so much, in fact, that He spoke of it to the crowd gathered
around Him. Would Jesus be surprised by *your* faith?

O Jesus, I have faith in You, but I want
even more. Increase my faith! Amen.

TRUSTING WHEN YOU'RE AFRAID

When I am afraid, I will trust in You. I praise the
Word of God. I have put my trust in God. I will
not be afraid. What can only a man do to me?

PSALM 56:3–4

✳

David had many powerful enemies, and he was often tempted
to lose hope. He didn't say that he was never afraid, because
that wasn't true. There were times, when war was near and
his armies were vastly outnumbered, that David was afraid.
But his key to success was this: "When I am afraid, I will
trust in You." When he trusted that God would be with him,
David's courage returned and he could say, "I will not be
afraid." Most of us today don't have enemies who want to
kill us, but the idea that helped David survive three thousand
years ago works just as well for us today.

God, in You I trust, and I will not be afraid.
Trusting You is the key to overcoming my
fear. Trusting You makes me strong. Yes,
God, I put my trust in You. Amen.

Night 236
ASK JESUS

They were surprised and wondered how easy
it was for Peter and John to speak. They could
tell they were men who had not gone to school.
But they knew they had been with Jesus.

ACTS 4:13

In Bible times, the priests and the Sadducees were among the most-educated men around and probably thought themselves the wisest. Yet, here were two uneducated men, Peter and John, speaking about Jesus and leaving them lost for words. It was Jesus who opened their minds to what was real in the world! Unlike Peter and John, we don't get to be with Jesus face-to-face, but we do get to invite Him into our lives, and with Him comes the kind of understanding He gave Peter and John. So, when you are faced with a problem, consider not only what you've learned in books and school and what others think you should do. Ask Jesus what to do.

Jesus, my teacher, how wonderful it is that You are willing and eager to share Your wisdom with me. Amen.

Night 237
JESUS' HELPER

"He must become more important.
I must become less important."

JOHN 3:30

✳

When John's disciples complained that a new preacher, Jesus, was drawing followers from their group, John said, "He must become more important. I must become less important." John understood that his job was to prepare the way for the Messiah. Maybe you feel like you're not good enough to be one of Jesus' helpers. Not everyone can preach. . .but there are so many other things that you can do. Be kind to everyone. Give food or clothing to the poor. Pray for others. Every time you help someone, you act as Jesus' helper. Focus on Jesus. He wants to be greater—more important—than anything else in your life.

Lord, I am Your helper, ready and excited to serve.
Put me where You need me most. Amen.

Night 238
HOW ARE YOU LIVING?

You should think about the kind of life you are living.
2 PETER 3:11

✳

Second Peter 3:11 says you should think about the *kind* of life you are living. Are you living a life pleasing to God? Or would the way you live make Him shake His head and say, "Oh, no. I need to help this kid turn toward Me"? Everyone, kids *and* grown-ups, needs to think about how their lives look to God. At bedtime each night, take a few minutes to think about the way you lived that day. Are there a few things for which you need to ask God's forgiveness? Did you do something good for others? What can you do tomorrow that will please God? The more you think about these things, the more likely you will live in a way that makes the Lord happy.

. . . .

Dear God, I want to live a life that pleases You.
Please show me the way. Amen.

Night 239
WAITING FOR GOD
TO ANSWER

How long, O Lord? Will You forget me forever?
How long will You hide Your face from me?

PSALM 13:1

When King David wrote Psalm 13, his heart was filled with sadness. His enemies succeeded while David failed, and worse, they let him know that they were happy about it. And, as long and as hard as David prayed, God seemed to have left him alone. Have you ever felt that way? It's difficult to believe that God still loves you when your prayers go unanswered. But God asks us to wait for His answer and to trust that He will answer when the time is just right. While writing, David remembered this, and he ended his psalm with these words: "But I have trusted in Your loving-kindness. My heart will be full of joy because You will save me" (v. 5).

Father, I know that You will never leave
me alone and afraid. I trust You. Amen.

Night 240
CROSSING THE FINISH LINE

*I have fought the good fight, I have
finished the race, I have kept the faith.*
2 TIMOTHY 4:7 NIV

In 1992, Derek Redmond was determined to win the Olympic 400-meter dash. But less than halfway around the track, his hamstring tore. His father ran out onto the track to help his son cross the finish line. In his moment of need, he didn't have to depend on his own strength; he leaned on his father. Our lives are like a race. We might set out with our eyes on a prize. But there are traps and obstacles along the way. Our faith will take a beating—it might be in shreds as we approach the end. We might have to hobble, hop, and crawl, but we know this—leaning on our Father, God, is our guarantee of crossing the finish line.

Lord, I've done my best. There's such a short
distance to cross that line. Carry me, please;
I can't get there on my own. Amen.

IMPORTANT TO JESUS

Then little children were brought to Him that He might put His hands on them and pray for them. The followers spoke sharp words to them. But Jesus said, "Let the little children come to Me. Do not stop them. The holy nation of heaven is made up of ones like these."

MATTHEW 19:13 14

Everyone crowded around Jesus. They wanted healing, and they wanted Him to pray for their needs. One by one, Jesus put His hands on them and prayed. Some mothers had brought their children to see Jesus. They wanted Him to bless their little ones. But when they tried to get through the crowds, some of Jesus' followers told them to go away. In the middle of that big crowd of people, Jesus saw what was happening. He called out, "Let the little children come to Me. Do not stop them." Kids are important to Jesus. They always have been and always will be. Jesus is never too busy to spend time with you and hear your prayers.

Dear Jesus, You always have time for me.
Thank You, Jesus. I love You! Amen.

THE WHOLE WORLD NEEDS TO KNOW

Then Eliakim. . .said to Rabshakeh, "Speak to your servants in the Aramaic language, for we understand it. Do not speak with us in the language of Judah. The people on the wall might hear it."

2 KINGS 18:26

✳

This verse might be confusing unless you focus on the idea of language. In this time of ancient kings, the rich and important spoke Aramaic, while the lower class—the people sitting on the wall—spoke Hebrew. What good was it to the lower class if the ancient Old Testament writings weren't translated into their language? Over thousands of years, the Bible has been translated into thousands of languages. But, even so, several hundred of those don't include *all* the books of the Bible. And millions of people today do not have a single verse of the Bible translated into their language. Pray for those who still have not heard the complete Word of God.

God, please help get Bibles into the hands of all the people. Amen.

IF YOU BELIEVE

"For we must tell what we have seen and heard."

ACTS 4:20

One of the men speaking here is Peter. He is talking to the religious leaders in the same temple where, a short time before, he had denied that he knew Jesus. Now Peter stands there, accusing the priests of the murder of his Lord. He isn't scared, and he isn't backing down. The Peter who denied Christ would never have spoken like this to the priests if he didn't know that Jesus had sent him help. The Holy Spirit, the Helper, was behind, around, and inside Peter. Our world can be troublesome. Sometimes you might be afraid. But if you believe that the Holy Spirit is always in and around you, you can stand up to anyone—or anything.

I believe it, Jesus! You are the Son of God, the risen Christ, the one who sent the Helper through whom I have strength to carry out God's will. Amen.

Night 244
GOD NEVER LEAVES

"Be strong and have strength of heart. Do not be afraid or shake with fear because of them. For the Lord your God is the One Who goes with you. He will be faithful to you. He will not leave you alone."

DEUTERONOMY 31:6

✳

This is part of a speech that Moses delivered to the Israelites just before they entered Canaan, the Promised Land. The Israelites worried that fighting might occur with the Canaanites. But Moses encouraged them to be strong and trust that the Lord would protect them. Many times, Moses reminded the Israelites that they needed to trust in God. God's words are even repeated in the New Testament in Hebrews 13:5: "I will never leave you or let you be alone." Even today, trouble exists in the part of the world known as the Promised Land. But God continues to promise the Israelites—and us too—"I will never leave you or let you be alone."

O God, You are the one who gives me courage when I am afraid. Thank You for promising to never leave me. Amen.

So Ananias went to that house. He put his
hands on Saul and said, "Brother Saul,
the Lord Jesus has sent me to you."

ACTS 9:17

Ananias was afraid to meet Saul. Saul (later known as Paul)
had murdered Christians—until Jesus visited him on the
road to Damascus. To Ananias, Paul must have seemed a
wild and extremely dangerous man. But because Jesus was
now in Paul's heart, the first word Ananias spoke to Paul
was *brother*. How can people so different from us ever be
called our "brother" or "sister"? Maybe you know someone
very different from you—maybe it has even made you avoid
that person. No doubt, Ananias felt the same about Paul.
But we need to look at others through Jesus' eyes and treat
everyone with loving-kindness. Why? Because we are all
God's children!

Lord, open my eyes to see how other kids and I
are alike. Help me to love them because we are all
brothers and sisters in God's big family. Amen.

Night 246

"FEEL" YOUR WORDS

The Lord said, "These people show respect to Me with their mouth, and honor Me with their lips, but their heart is far from Me. Their worship of Me is worth nothing. They teach rules that men have made."

ISAIAH 29:13

Are there certain prayers that you recite at mealtime, at bedtime, or in church? When was the last time you really thought about those words and what they mean? From God's viewpoint, the actions of our hearts speak louder than our words. If our prayers consist of mindlessly repeating words, then we are missing out on connecting with our God, who loves us and wants a relationship with us through our praying. In other words, God wants us to be thinking of Him and loving Him when we pray. When you pray, remember that God is listening. The next time you recite a prayer from memory, think about its words. Feel them and speak them from your heart.

Father, thank You for reminding me to think about my prayers. When I pray a familiar prayer, I will pray from my heart. Amen.

Night 247
JESUS LOVES SINNERS

But God showed His love to us. While we
were still sinners, Christ died for us.

ROMANS 5:8

※

If you read the Old Testament, you'll discover that time
after time, from the very beginning, people turned against
God and did what was wrong. And still, God loved us all
so much that He sent His only Son to die for us, a bunch of
sinners. No, we didn't deserve Jesus. But He gave His life for
us anyway. We will continue to sin, and God will continue
to forgive us and love us, thanks to Jesus. What can we do
to show Jesus our appreciation? When someone asks for
help, we can lend a hand readily and without complaining.
Maybe that person doesn't deserve our help. But we should
help anyway, remembering that Jesus helped us, a bunch
of sinners.

• •

Jesus, You generously gave Your life for me—
someone undeserving of Your sacrifice. When
someone who I feel is undeserving asks for my help,
I will remember what You did for me. Amen.

Night 248
STORM CLOUDS

The Lord is slow to anger and great in power.
The Lord will be sure to punish the guilty.
The way He punishes is in the strong-wind and
storm. The clouds are the dust under His feet.

NAHUM 1:3

Storm clouds remind us of God's power. He commands
the raging winds, the crashing thunder, and the flashes of
lightning. Nahum 1:3 says, "The way He punishes is in the
strong-wind and storm." But God is very patient and slow to
punish His people. He waits for us to acknowledge Him as
our King and Savior and to ask for His forgiveness. Then He
welcomes us into His arms. Next time you look at the clouds,
remember they are just dust on God's feet. He towers high
above them, looking down at us from heaven.

Lord, I look up and see You in the clouds, the sunshine,
and the stars. What wonders lie beyond them?
Someday I will see You in heaven. Amen.

Night 249
AVOID THE TRAP

Do not have anything to do with a man given to anger,
or go with a man who has a bad temper. Or you
might learn his ways and get yourself into a trap.

PROVERBS 22:24–25

Proverbs 22:24–25 says not to hang with angry people. But you could substitute the word *anger* with any other sin. In other words, you should choose your friends wisely and stay away from those who willingly do what is wrong. It can be easy to fall into a trap. For example: if someone speaks angry words to you, then you might speak angry words back. King Solomon, the author of Proverbs 22, says we shouldn't hang out with people who are always angry or those who behave badly. Their behavior can be contagious, like a cold or the flu. Wise words from a very wise king!

Heavenly Father, please help me to choose friends who
love You and do their best to live by Your rules. Amen.

Night 250
YOUR BEST FOR GOD

I do not understand myself. I want to do what is right
but I do not do it. Instead, I do the very thing I hate.

ROMANS 7:15

People get it into their heads that they need to be perfect
or do things perfectly. With those thoughts in mind, when
they don't live up to their own expectations, they feel like
failures. Paul was one of Jesus' strongest followers, and yet
he thought of himself as a failure. When he wrote the words
in today's verse, he hated it that as much as he loved God,
he still continued to sin. Paul also wrote, "There is not one
person who is right with God. No, not even one!" (3:10). "For
all. . .have sinned and have missed the shining-greatness
of God" (3:23). No one is perfect. No one can be perfect.
So stop being hard on yourself. Your best is good enough.

I struggle with perfection, Lord. I try my best and
still I fail. But my best is good enough for You!
Teach me not to be so hard on myself. Amen.

Night 251
GOD, THE CREATOR

The heavens are telling of the greatness of God and the great open spaces above show the work of His hands.

PSALM 19:1

＊

The first verse of the Bible clearly states that God created the universe. Scientific observations agree that our universe did indeed have a beginning. But science goes much deeper: it shows an earth fine-tuned for intelligent life, an amazingly rare possibility even in the vastness of space. The evidence points to a planet designed by a Creator. With the heavens displaying the Creator's glory, it shouldn't surprise us that scientists also discovered that the conditions that make life possible on Earth provide a perfect setting to study our universe as well. Stand outside on a clear night and look into the sky. Think about the magnificence and greatness of God's creation.

. . . .

Father, I see what Your mighty hands have made, nothing out of place, the whole universe in line with Your perfect will. You are so awesome! Amen.

Night 252
INCREASE YOUR FAITH

For this reason, we always pray for you.
We pray that our God will make you worth being
chosen. We pray that His power will help you
do the good things you want to do. We pray
that your work of faith will be complete.

2 THESSALONIANS 1:11

Paul spent much time praying for his friends in various churches. For the Thessalonians, he prayed that God would make them worth being chosen. In other words, give them all they needed to do what God wanted them to do. Paul's words suggest that his friends already had in mind their calling—God's plan for them. He asked that God use His power to help the Thessalonians stay strong in their faith and keep working toward their goal. God has a plan for everyone, and through His power God helps us to complete His plan. When you pray tonight, ask God to increase your faith so you can do the good things God has planned for you to do.

By faith, I believe that You will fulfill the plans
You have for me. Thank You, Father! Amen.

Night 253
A GREAT PRIZE

For I know that nothing can keep us from the love
of God. Death cannot! Life cannot! Angels cannot!
Leaders cannot! Any other power cannot!

ROMANS 8:38

Lots of things try to separate us from God—way more things
than you can think of. Why? Because God's love is a great
prize! Otherwise, no one on this earth (or below it) would
care.

Jesus warned us. He said, "In the world you will have much
trouble" (John 16:33). And then He added this comforting
thought: "But take hope! I have power over the world!" It's
a tough battle to stand firm against trouble, but in Romans
8:38 39, Paul tells us to stay strong. If you'll only hold on
to Jesus, He'll wrap His arms *and His love* around you. Any
trouble you can think of—earthquakes, meteor strikes, storms,
whatever!—can never break His embrace.

Wrap Your strong arms around me, Jesus. Embrace
me in love whenever evil tries to separate us. I know
that I will be safe resting in Your arms. Amen.

Night 254
HIDING GOD'S WORD IN YOUR HEART

Your Word have I hid in my heart,
that I may not sin against You.
PSALM 119:11

God allowed Jesus to be tempted by Satan, but He didn't give in, because the Word of God was in His heart. Each time Satan tempted Him, Jesus was able to keep trouble away by using God's Word as a weapon. This same weapon is available to us today. By reading and thinking about God's Word, we become much stronger in our faith. It becomes easier to battle temptation. The Bible says that we will never be tempted beyond that which we are able to handle (1 Corinthians 10:13). And Psalm 119:11 reminds us that we can win against temptation by filling our hearts and minds with God's Word.

Dear God, when I face trouble, I will rely on Your Word. I will find comfort, refreshment, and strength in its everlasting power. Amen.

Night 255
IDOLS

And he broke in pieces the brass snake that Moses
had made. For until those days the people of Israel
burned special perfume to it. It was called Nehushtan.

2 KINGS 18:4

✳

The Israelites became impatient with Moses and God and
complained bitterly against them, so God sent poisonous
snakes that bit many of them. When the people said they
were sorry, God told Moses to hammer out a bronze snake
and hold it up on a pole, and "if a snake bit any man, he
would live when he looked at the brass snake" (Numbers
21:9). The Israelites hung on to this symbol of God's power
for hundreds of years. And eventually, the Israelites began to
worship the bronze snake. God gives us many good things,
but if we begin to give them too much of our attention, they
become idols and we should get rid of them.

Heavenly Father, I'm grateful for the good things You
have given me, but open my eyes if I have turned any
of them into idols. I want to worship only You. Amen.

Night 256
PERFECT IN EVERY WAY

Now that which we see is as if we were looking in a broken mirror. But then we will see everything. Now I know only a part. But then I will know everything in a perfect way. That is how God knows me right now.

1 CORINTHIANS 13:12

✳

Some carnivals and fairs have fun houses with mirrors that make your reflection look strange. They might make you extremely tall or wide or even wiggly. In 1 Corinthians 13:12, Paul says we see the world as if we are looking into a broken mirror. He meant that we can't see the world through God's eyes and know everything about it perfectly, the way God does. We can't even know everything about ourselves the way that God does. But Paul adds that when we get to heaven, then we will see things with godly eyes. Imagine how perfect, beautiful, and wonderful everything will look. Then we will see ourselves the way God made us—perfect in every way.

God, I'm looking forward to heaven someday so I can see things the way that You do. Amen.

The Lord said to Moses, "Say to the people
of Israel, 'These are the special suppers
of the Lord, which you will keep for holy
meetings. These are My special suppers.' "

LEVITICUS 23:1–2

Holidays ("special suppers") in ancient Israel combined celebrations with worship to honor God's amazing blessings. The weekly Sabbath, although a day for rest and worship, served as a time for Israelites to remember that God had saved them from slavery in Egypt (Deuteronomy 5:15). At the feast of harvest, or Pentecost, loaves of bread were presented as an offering from the wheat harvest, along with sacrificial animals. Jewish tradition also links this feast to the day God gave Moses the Ten Commandments on Mount Sinai. Like the Israelites, we should use all our holidays to celebrate God's goodness and remember the blessings He has given us.

Father, I'm sorry that so many people forget
to honor You on holidays. I will remember to
worship You on holidays and every day! Amen.

Night 258
BLIND HEARTS SEE

The eyes of those who do not believe are made
blind by Satan who is the god of this world.
He does not want the light of the Good News to
shine in their hearts. This Good News shines as
the shining-greatness of Christ. Christ is as God is.

2 CORINTHIANS 4:4

The idea that some people can't understand the gospel breaks
the Lord's heart. But there is something that we can do! We
can show nonbelievers who Jesus is through our words and
actions. We can make them notice that we are always kind,
even when others are not kind back. We can speak softly
and gently and avoid getting angry. In other words, we can
do our best to be like Jesus and hope they will see. God is
more powerful than Satan! He has a way of making blind
hearts see. And often He uses us—His children—to open a
nonbeliever's eyes.

Heavenly Father, even where my faith is not welcomed,
I will honor You and do my best to be like Jesus. Amen.

Night 259
HOLY ANGER

They turned away from the Lord and did not serve
Him. The anger of the Lord was against Israel.

JUDGES 10:6–7

✳

Does God get angry? Yes, He does. But His is a holy anger against evil. From the beginning of time, God has expressed His anger against all forms of wickedness and idol worship. But—think about this—His anger toward evil is also an expression of love for those of us who are good and love Him. Anger is best left to God. Paul taught believers, "If you are angry, do not let it become sin. . . . Do not let the devil start working in your life" (Ephesians 4:26–27). If you become angry, get over it! Let God deal with your problem before Satan sneaks in and makes you do something you'll regret.

Help me to control my anger so I will
not sin. Thank You, Lord. Amen.

Night 260
SUFFERING FOR JESUS

So the missionaries went away from the court happy that they could suffer shame because of His Name.

ACTS 5:41

*

The missionaries mentioned in this verse were Jesus' disciples. Those in the ancient Jewish court didn't like all the attention the disciples got. So they arrested the men and punished them with a whipping. Then they let them go and told them to stop speaking about the Lord. As the disciples limped away in pain, they rejoiced that God had allowed them to suffer for Him. The Bible says, "But even if you should suffer for what is right, you are blessed" (1 Peter 3:14 NIV). God sees, and He will bless you for doing what is right. Even if someone makes fun of you, stand strong for Jesus. God will see and bless you.

• •

Dear Jesus, sometimes I am bullied because of my Christian faith. Surely You understand how that feels. Help me to have courage and focus on Your blessings. Amen.

STRENGTH IN WEAKNESS

He answered me, "I am all you need. I give
you My loving-favor. My power works best in
weak people." I am happy to be weak and have
troubles so I can have Christ's power in me.

2 CORINTHIANS 12:9

✳

Eric Liddell was a missionary to China. He wrote a prayer
telling God that whatever terrible things happened to him,
he would not lose his faith. He didn't mention that he was in
a Japanese prison camp, not knowing if his family was safe,
and that he was dying of a brain tumor. But Eric's certainty
that God loved him—and that Jesus died for him—was enough
to prove that his blessings still outweighed his problems.
Eric's story reminds us that our bad times don't have to be
hopeless times. When we are weak, God can still do great
things through us.

Lord, in my weakness You give me strength,
and You are my comfort in times of trouble.
With You in my heart, I have all that I need. Amen.

Night 262
IN GOD'S HANDS

*The Lord was sorry that He had made man
on the earth. He had sorrow in His heart.*
GENESIS 6:6

God did everything possible to avoid the flood. He gave people plenty of time to turn from their wickedness. He patiently waited until there was only one good man left—Noah. God didn't send the flood without warning. Noah warned the world for a hundred years (the time it took the ark to be built), but no one believed him. By the time the rain began, the world was out of control with sin. No one cared about God. God was sorry that His people had filled His world with sin. God is good to those who love Him. So good that He sent Jesus to save us from sin. The Bible gives us every reason to put our whole life into His hands, today and forever.

My loving and forgiving God, You knew that humans would continue to sin, so You sent Jesus to save us. Your love for us is greater than any other love! Amen.

Night 263
SHINE ON!

Nothing should be done because of pride
or thinking about yourself. Think of other
people as more important than yourself.

PHILIPPIANS 2:3

Jesus didn't dress in fancy clothes. He looked just like an ordinary guy dressed in a robe and sandals. But when people looked at Jesus, they saw love. They saw it in how He looked at them, the way He spoke to them, and even how He said their names. Those who met Jesus during the short time He was on the earth must have truly been filled with His love. The proof of this is the huge crowds that followed Him. The people knew that Jesus truly cared about them and would heal and help them. The way Jesus behaved made every person feel important. And that is how we should behave too. With everyone you meet, let the love of Jesus shine through you.

Jesus, I want to be like You. Extend Your love to others through my smile, my words, and my acts. Amen.

Night 264
GREAT AND WONDERFUL THINGS

"Call to Me, and I will answer you. And I will show you great and wonderful things which you do not know."

JEREMIAH 33:3

✳

This verse is the Word of God speaking directly to the prophet Jeremiah. For forty years, Jeremiah had been sharing God's warning that the cities of Judah and Jerusalem would be destroyed because of their people's sin. Now, God's, and Jeremiah's, words were coming true: the Babylonian army was ready to attack. King Zedekiah, Judah's king, accused Jeremiah of siding with the Babylonians and had him thrown into prison. But while Jeremiah was there, God told him to pray. If we pray to God, He will answer us and "show [us] great and wonderful things which [we] do not know." Just as God gave Jeremiah wisdom, He will do the same for you.

God, I need Your help. I've been struggling with a problem, and I'm still not sure what to do. But You know! Please, God, guide me with Your wisdom. Amen.

Night 265
EVERYTHING YOU NEED

"It is bad for you who are rich. You are receiving all that you will get."

LUKE 6:24

Jesus reminded rich people that everything they owned on earth was short-lived. In other words, they couldn't take their wealth with them to heaven. And forever life in heaven is worth far more than anything on earth. Jesus' message is for all people. Be content with what you have (Hebrews 13:5). "Do not gather together for yourself riches of this earth. . . . Gather together riches in heaven where they will not be eaten by bugs or become rusted. Men cannot break in and steal them" (Matthew 6:19–20). Remember: if you have Jesus and His promise of forever life, then you have everything you need.

Lord Jesus, thank You for Your many blessings.
I am grateful for them all, but nothing
compares to my relationship with You.
It is always first in my heart. Amen.

Night 266
UNLIKELY PEOPLE

As Jesus went from there, He saw a man called
Matthew. Matthew was sitting at his work
gathering taxes. Jesus said to him, "Follow
Me." Matthew got up and followed Jesus.

MATTHEW 9:9

God often uses the most unlikely people to carry out His
plans. Jesus chose the unlikely to be His disciples. At least
seven were fishermen. Jesus said He would make them fishers
of men, meaning that He had chosen them to gather other
people to follow Him. And Jesus chose Matthew, a tax col-
lector, who worked in a business known to take advantage
of people and their money. And Judas Iscariot. . .Jesus chose
him, knowing that Judas would betray Him and turn Him
over to soldiers to die on the cross. We might not always
understand why God uses unlikely people to do His work,
but we can trust that He knows what He's doing. Pray and
ask Him to lead you too.

God, You know the plans You have for me.
How can I serve You? Show me the way. Amen.

Night 267
NO ONE BUT GOD

When Peter came, Cornelius got down at his
feet and worshiped him. But Peter raised him up
and said, "Get up! I am just a man like you."

ACTS 10:25–26

After Jesus rose from the dead and the disciples were filled
with the Holy Spirit, Peter became a powerhouse and a miracle worker. He prayed, and the sick were healed, and the
dead were raised to life. Even his shadow healed people! (See
Acts 3:1–8; 5:15; 9:32–42.) So, when Peter entered Cornelius'
house, this Roman soldier bowed down to worship him.
Peter quickly grabbed Cornelius, pulled him to his feet, and
set him straight—he was to bow down and worship no one
but God! This is good advice for us when we're tempted to
bow to and worship an entertainer, a sports figure, or any
other person. God is the only one worthy of our worship.

Father, You are my only God, and I worship
only You. I will not bow down to any
person or anything on earth. Amen.

THE HEALTHIEST FOOD WE CAN EAT

Then He said to me, "Son of man, eat what is in front of you. Eat this book, then go and speak to the people of Israel."

EZEKIEL 3:1

God wasn't *really* telling the prophet Ezekiel to start chomping on the book set before him. The "book" was the Word of God, the scriptures, and God wanted Ezekiel to know very well what God wanted him to say to the Israelites. God's message to them was in that book (back then, a scroll) set before him.

God's Word, the Bible, is the healthiest "food" we can "eat." Its words give us energy and strength. The Bible brings us joy, life, hope, peace, comfort, encouragement, and so much more. It also helps us to share the good news of Jesus. Have you "eaten" God's Word today?

Give me strength and energy with Your Word, God. Fill me up with Your scriptures. Amen.

Night 269
GET UP AND GET BUSY

"Do something to let me see that you have turned from your sins. Do not begin to say to yourselves, 'We have Abraham as our father.' I tell you, God can make children for Abraham out of these stones."

LUKE 3:8

To understand this verse, you need to remember God's promise to Abraham: "I will give you many children. . . . You will be the father of many nations. . . . I will make My agreement between Me and you and your children after you. . . . I will be God to you and to your children's children after you" (Genesis 17:2, 4, 7). God honored His promise. But, after a while, the Israelites thought they were more important than other people. They became lazy, and their faith in God was weak. It was John the Baptist, many, many generations later, who spoke the words in Luke 3:8, warning God's people to get up and get busy working for the Lord. Are you working for Jesus?

Jesus, put me to work. What can I do to spread Your Word? I am ready and willing. Amen.

Night 270

NOTHING CAN STOP GOD'S PLANS

Now there was no one to be found in all the land of
Israel who made things of iron. . . . So each one of the
Israelites went down to the Philistines to get his plow,
his pick, his ax, or his grain cutter sharpened. . . .
So on the day of battle there was no sword or spear in
the hands of any of the people who were with Saul and
Jonathan. But Saul and his son Jonathan had them.

1 SAMUEL 13:19–20, 22

✳

Technology in Old Testament days was all about who
had the strongest spears and swords. The Philistines
planned to use their advanced technology in metalworking
against the Israelites. But God had another plan. Surprisingly,
not much has changed since then. Nations still compete
for the best technology and use their technology against
other nations. The lesson is that even the most advanced
twenty-first-century technology can't stop God's plans.
Just as He provided for the Israelites to win their battle
back then, He provides for us now.

How great You are, Lord! Amen.

Night 271
A SHIFT IN PRIORITIES

"No one can have two bosses. He will hate the one and love the other. Or he will listen to the one and work against the other. You cannot have both God and riches as your boss at the same time."

MATTHEW 6:24

Jesus reminds us that we should use our possessions and money for God's purpose. If we let our stuff be our boss, then we'll have no time or space in our hearts for God. Some of the things we think are important—family, friends, pets, school, hobbies, and games—are good things, but we place them out of order in our priorities. God is our boss. The boss above all other bosses! And He wants to be number one in our hearts. So when you find your stuff getting in between you and God, stand up to it and say, "Hey! You're not the boss of me!"

God, I am so busy with school, friends, and other things that often my priorities shift away from You. I'm sorry. I will try to do better. Amen.

FRUITS OF THE SPIRIT

But the fruit that comes from having the Holy Spirit in our lives is: love, joy, peace, not giving up, being kind, being good, having faith, being gentle, and being the boss over our own desires. The Law is not against these things.

GALATIANS 5:22–23

The Galatians had been trying to follow the laws set forth in the Old Testament. While there was nothing wrong with that, they were forgetting that Jesus came to save them from the sins they committed. Paul reminded them that Jesus was more important than the Law. When the Holy Spirit lives inside someone, it shows on the outside through how that person behaves. Paul calls those behaviors the "fruit" of the Holy Spirit. Love, joy, peace, not giving up, being kind, being good, having faith, being gentle, and being the boss over our own wants are the fruits of the Spirit. Does the Holy Spirit live in your heart? How do you know?

God, I want the way I behave to show the world that the Holy Spirit lives in my heart. Amen.

Night 273
THE ONLY WAY

If a man has not worked to be saved, but has put his trust in God Who saves men from the punishment of their sins, that man is made right with God because of his trust in God.

ROMANS 4:5

This verse reminds us that God does not provide a ticket to heaven based on good work. Still, people think they will get to heaven through working hard! They say, "I've worked hard at being a good person. I hope God will let me into heaven." It isn't about work—trusting Jesus is *the only way* to get to heaven. A person can do good work, but if they have not accepted Jesus as their Savior, then they won't get there. Work to please God, yes, but remember that the only thing that will get you into heaven is trusting your Savior, Jesus.

Jesus, I understand that the only way to heaven is by believing in You and Your gift of salvation. Thank You for leading me there. Amen.

GOD IS OUR EVERYTHING

My body and my heart may grow weak, but God is the strength of my heart and all I need forever.

PSALM 73:26

✳

Asaph is the man who wrote Psalm 73. He was King David's music director and author of twelve of the psalms. In Psalm 73, Asaph wonders, *If God is good, then why do some good people suffer and some bad people don't?* Asaph confesses that he sometimes feels like giving up and joining the bad guys (vv. 2–3). Asaph cries out to God. In prayer, he realizes that while the bad might do well for a while, God will punish them in His own way and in His own time. Asaph ends up praising God, "[You are] the strength of my heart and all I need forever." When we feel like giving up, Psalm 73:26 reminds us that God is our everything.

Help me to be patient when seeking punishment for the bad guys. In Your time, Lord, and in Your way, You will deal with them. Amen.

Night 275
PASSING THE TEST

Put yourselves through a test. See if you belong
to Christ. Then you will know you belong to
Christ, unless you do not pass the test.

2 CORINTHIANS 13:5

Hanging out with other Christians is important. When you
are with them, you feel comfortable talking about Jesus and
praying and sharing your faith with one another. But what
happens when you step outside that comfort zone and you
find yourself in a crowd of nonbelievers? Satan will do his
best to try and trick you into doing what you know is wrong.
Ask yourself, "Would Jesus approve?" If you answer yes,
then you've passed the faith test. But if your answer is no,
you've failed. Everyone fails the test sometimes. The good
news is you can take the test again and again. If you open
your heart to Jesus, then He will strengthen your faith and
help you to pass.

Jesus, whenever I head the wrong way,
pull me back. My heart is open to You.
Please boost my faith and make it strong. Amen.

Night 276
BE CAREFUL

Be careful that no one changes your mind and faith by much learning and big sounding ideas. Those things are what men dream up. They are always trying to make new religions. These leave out Christ.

COLOSSIANS 2:8

God's Word is perfectly perfect. That's why memorizing scripture word for word is important. When you do that and learn the true meaning of God's words, then you are less likely to fall into Satan's trap. Satan was the serpent who convinced Adam and Eve that it was okay if they ate fruit from the one tree God said was forbidden. Because they listened to what they thought was good advice, sin came into the world forever! So be careful that no one changes your mind about what God's Word says. Ask Jesus to help you decide whether what you hear is real and true.

Dear Lord, keep me focused on the truth of Your Word. Remind me to study the Bible and trust You to help me understand it. Amen.

ONLY ONE GOD

"But where are your gods that you made for yourself?
Let them come if they can save you when you are in
trouble. For you have as many gods as cities, O Judah."

JEREMIAH 2:28

The Bible has much to say about false gods. In the first of His
Ten Commandments, God said, "Have no gods other than Me"
(Exodus 20:3). But the people didn't listen. Even while Moses
was up on Mount Sinai receiving the Ten Commandments
from God, the Israelites were worshipping a calf made of
gold. Because Moses had been gone from them so long,
they had lost faith in God and in Moses—and they made
their own god to worship. Even today, people worship false
gods money, celebrities, things. But there is only one God,
and He demands our attention.

Father, many things distract our attention from
You—the internet, TV, books. Open my eyes to false
gods. The only God I want to worship is You! Amen.

Night 278
DAY OF REST

Jesus said to them, "The Day of Rest was made for the good of man. Man was not made for the Day of Rest."

MARK 2:27

✳

In His fourth commandment, God said, "Remember the Day of Rest, to keep it holy. Six days you will do all your work. But the seventh day is a Day of Rest to the Lord your God" (Exodus 20:8–10). God's reason for this command is found in Genesis 2:2–3: "On the seventh day God ended His work. . . . And He rested. . . . Then God honored the seventh day and made it holy, because in it He rested." If the Creator took a day off for rest after six days of creation work, who are we to ignore His command that we rest too? How does your family honor Sunday? Make it a day of rest—a day in which you remember and honor God.

Lord, in our family, Sunday will be a day of rest and remembrance of You. Show us ways that we, as a family, can honor this day and spend it with You. Amen.

Night 279
THE BEST WAY TO START YOUR DAY

In the morning, O Lord, You will hear my voice. In the morning I will lay my prayers before You and will look up.

PSALM 5:3

God loves hearing your voice as you go about your day. He wants you to speak to Him when you are in school. Invite Him to give you wisdom when you take a test. Ask Him to provide you with understanding in math, science, or any subject you struggle with. Speak to God when you play sports. Ask for physical strength and for Him to help you be a good sport. Get in the habit of looking around and thanking God for all the blessings you see. Psalm 5:3 reminds us that it's important to start every day with some quiet time with God. Beginning tomorrow, get up a little earlier than usual and start your day with the Father. He's waiting to hear from you.

Dear God, thank You for listening to my prayers and knowing exactly what I need. I will meet You in the morning so we can talk before I start my day. Amen.

Do you think I am trying to get the favor of men,
or of God? If I were still trying to please men,
I would not be a servant owned by Christ.

GALATIANS 1:10

✳

Everyone loves a happy ending, but the truth is that in this world, some endings aren't happy. Parents divorce, people die, dreams don't always come true, and those who are supposed to love us sometimes let us down. But the good news? There is someone out there who makes our happily-ever-after a reality—Jesus! He loves us all the time, no matter what. He can heal broken relationships and comfort us when we are sad. He knows our dreams. When we focus on Jesus, He makes all the world's problems seem easier to handle. And when He died for us, He gave us the most special gift of all—the gift of happily-ever-after in heaven.

. . . .

Jesus, You must really love me to have
suffered and given Your life for me. You loved
me before any human did, and Your love for
me lasts forever. I love You too. Amen.

Night 281
KNOWING JESUS

*Jesus Christ is the same yesterday
and today and forever.*
HEBREWS 13:8

✳

Close your eyes and imagine Jesus when He was on earth. What do you think He looked like? We can only guess. There were no cameras back then, and the men who wrote the Bible did not include drawings of Jesus. But what Jesus looked like is not at all important when compared to who Jesus is: God's Son, the Savior, the Messiah—the one God sent to earth to die for our sins.

The Jesus who lived back then is the same now, and He will be forever! Jesus spoke the truth, and His truth lives on in the Bible and in us. Jesus is, and forever He will be, and all that He was and is. . .is yours! Isn't that awesome?

Dear Jesus, I've come to know You through
the Bible, and I'm grateful that You won't ever
change. I know I can always count on You,
because the Bible tells me so. Amen.

Night 282
LIFE GOES ON

Jesus said, "I am the Way and the Truth and the Life. No one can go to the Father except by Me."

JOHN 14:6

Jesus is our way to heaven—our *only* way! His death on the cross cleared a path for us that wasn't there until Jesus arrived. Until He came, no one had a sin-free heart pure enough for heaven. Everything Jesus said here on earth was the truth. And we can count on His words in the Bible being 100 percent true, now and forever. It is Jesus who took the punishment for our sins so our hearts will be pure and ready for heaven. He is our promise that life goes on for Christians when they die—eternal life, *forever* life, in heaven. And when you get to heaven, it is Jesus who will take you by the hand and introduce you to the one who made you.

• •

You mean everything to me, Jesus.
Without You, I would be totally lost. Amen.

Night 283
GOD IS A BIG GOD

Great is our Lord, and great in power.
His understanding has no end.

PSALM 147:5

✳

Psalm 147:4 says God knows the exact number of stars. And there's more. God calls every one of them by name—as if they were His pets! Remember that the next time you wonder if God is big enough to answer your prayers. The second half of this verse says God's "understanding has no end." When you are praying for wisdom in a complicated or worrisome situation, fix that thought firmly in your mind. You may have no clue what the right answer is, but God certainly does! His understanding is endless. Psalm 147:5 is one of the most powerful verses in the Bible. When we think deeply about its words, they can fill our minds with comfort and peace.

• •

God, who am I among all the stars in the universe? But You know their names, and You know mine too! You know me, You understand me, and that brings me peace. Amen.

Night 284
LOVE WINS!

When they say, "He went up," what does it mean but that He had first gone down to the deep parts of the earth?

EPHESIANS 4:9

In World War II, paratroopers jumped out of planes in the dark of night into enemy territory. Imagine this: Your enemy controls the land below. On the way down, the jumpmaster takes away all your weapons. He says there are some good people below who might help—though they don't have many weapons themselves. . .and you will definitely die. Would you make the jump? Jesus had to come down to earth—"enemy territory"—before He could complete God's plan of salvation and go back up to heaven to be with His Father. Jesus weighed all the risks of coming down to earth. He knew He would die. *But He loved us.* Love won—and down He came!

. . . .

Love came down. I will remember that, Jesus. Because You love me, You came down to save me. Thank You! Amen.

THE IMPORTANCE OF LISTENING

They. . .went up to the top of the hill country, saying,
"Here we are. It is true we have sinned. But we will
go up to the place which the Lord has promised."

NUMBERS 14:40

✳

Moses sent scouts to explore the land God had promised to
Israel. The men returned and reported, "The people living
there are powerful" (Numbers 13:28 NLT). Two scouts urged
the Israelites to go at once and take possession of the land.
But others spread fear, saying, "We can't go up against them!
They are stronger than we are!" (Numbers 13:31 NLT). Hearing
this, the Israelites turned against Moses. For their unbelief,
God sentenced the Israelites to wander forty years in the
desert. Ignoring God's words, the Israelites still tried to take
the land, but the enemy soundly defeated them. It's important
to listen for God's voice and act on His instructions.

Father, help me to always tune in to Your
words and follow Your instructions. Amen.

Night 286
THE PRIZE OF FOREVER LIFE

You know that only one person gets a crown
for being in a race even if many people run.
You must run so you will win the crown.

1 CORINTHIANS 9:24

✳

In his letter to the Corinthians, Paul compared living life the way Jesus wants us to with the intense training of runners. They keep their eyes on the goal and their minds on the commitment that helps them put one foot in front of the other, no matter what. Paul reminded the Corinthians that they should live as if running toward heaven as their goal. He told them to keep their minds on Jesus, because Jesus would give them the strength to work hard and keep their eyes on the prize. For runners in a race, the prize is a trophy, but the prize for living the way Jesus wants us to live is forever life in heaven—the greatest prize of all!

Jesus, please help me to work hard to live a good life
and to keep my eyes fixed on You and heaven. Amen.

YOUR WISH LIST

Take lies and what is false far from me. Do not let me be poor or rich. Feed me with the food that I need.

PROVERBS 30:8

In Proverbs 30 verses 7–8, a common man named Agur offered his "wish list" to God: "Two things I have asked of You. . . Take lies and what is false far from me. Do not let me be poor or rich. Feed me with the food that I need." He continued by saying a rich man was likely to take credit for his own success and forget God; but a poor man faced the temptation to steal to meet his needs (v. 9). Agur asked God to provide everything that he needed. What would be on your wish list to God? Would your wishes bring you closer to Him?

Dear God, guide me in the things I wish for. Lead me to ask only for those things that will strengthen my relationship with You. Amen.

LOVE COVERS ALL

Hate starts fights, but love covers all sins.
PROVERBS 10:12

The word *hate* appears in the Bible (NLV) 757 times—676 in the Old Testament, and 81 in the New Testament. The word even shows up in Genesis, the first book in the Bible, proof that hate has existed for a very long time. Throughout ancient times and today, people suffer because of hate. Hate seems to have taken over the world, but Proverbs 10:12 says that love covers all sins. And what is love? *God is love!* His love is more powerful than all that sinful hate, and love will win over hate every time. When you pray tonight, ask God to keep hate far from you. Ask Him to fill your heart with love and forgiveness, the same way that He loves you.

Father, help me not to fall into hate's sinful trap.
I want to always be loving and forgiving toward
others, the way that You are toward me. Amen.

ON TRACK WITH GOD

*After he had seen this, we agreed that God told us
to go to Macedonia to tell them the Good News.*

ACTS 16:10

✳

Missionaries Paul and Silas mapped out the route they
wanted to take. They traveled through Syria and into the
southern provinces of Asia Minor. But God stopped them
from preaching there. So, they traveled to their next desti-
nation—but God stopped them from preaching there too!
In a dream, a Macedonian man appeared to Paul saying,
"Come over to the country of Macedonia and help us!"
(Acts 16:9). Paul and Silas sailed to the region of Macedonia,
which was exactly where God wanted them! Do you listen
for God's direction in all areas of your life, or do you go
your own way? Seek His guidance and make adjustments
to stay on track with Him.

• •

*God, so often I go my own way and miss out
on Your best for me. Help me to listen for Your
guidance so I can stay on course. Amen.*

GOD'S THOUGHTS AND ADVICE

Greet Mary. She worked hard for you.

ROMANS 16:6

Some people wonder if the Bible is true or if it is some sort of ancient novel, a kind of fairy tale.

As you study the Bible and line up its events with history, you will discover facts that prove that the Bible is true. Think about this: If you wrote a novel, would you create multiple characters all with the same name? One proof that the Bible is a record of true-life events is how many people carry the same name: more than five are called Mary, at least three are James, three John, and two Judas! The Bible reads more like a history book than a novel. It is all about real people and events; and sprinkled throughout are God's thoughts and His advice to us. Read it and judge for yourself.

• •

Father, I believe the Bible as truth. Some people say that some or all of it is fiction. But I know better. The Bible is the Word of God. Amen.

Night 291
SHINING LIKE STARS

"Those who are wise will shine like the bright heavens. And those who lead many to do what is right and good will shine like the stars forever and ever."

DANIEL 12:3

✳

An angel appeared to Daniel and told him what would happen at a time far into the future. The angel said that, someday, the bodies of those who have died will rise up from the grave, like Jesus' body did! But not all people. . .only Christians who had lived their lives for God. Those who were wise in life and believed in Jesus will rise with beautiful new bodies that glow with light. Because they lived to please God and led others to do the same, they will shine like the stars, forever and ever. If we shine brightly for Jesus now, by doing our best to be like Him, then He will see to it that, someday, in our new bodies, we will shine brightly forever—like the stars!

Mighty God, I will lead others to Jesus, and together we will light the way to You and heaven. Amen.

Night 292
A RELATIONSHIP WITH JESUS

For if a man belongs to Christ, he is a new person.
The old life is gone. New life has begun.

2 CORINTHIANS 5:17

In today's Bible verse, Paul describes what happens to any person who enters into a relationship with Jesus. As soon as people accept Jesus into their hearts, it is as if their old lives are gone! All new believers begin learning how to live with Jesus ruling their hearts. They begin welcoming other Christians into their lives. They stop beating themselves up for mistakes they made in the past. They start to see themselves through God's eyes and love themselves the way that God loves them. They begin a lifetime of learning from and living by God's Word. You can help others to give up their old lives and get a fresh start. Tell them about Jesus!

Jesus, my Savior, You've made me brand-new,
and I thank You! I want to help others get a
new life too. Please teach me how. Amen.

MUSTARD SEEDS

"It is the smallest of seeds. But when it is
full-grown, it is larger than the grain of
the fields and it becomes a tree."

MATTHEW 13:32

✳

Jesus picked up the tiniest of all seeds—a mustard seed—to
show His disciples. Once planted, the seed grows slowly. The
seedling takes days or even weeks before it gives any sign
of breaking through the ground. Why does it take so long
to grow? A mustard plant requires deep roots. The plant
grows its roots three times faster than the stalk in order to
be well grounded. Mustard trees grow up to twenty-one
feet tall with the roots reaching down to sixty-three feet
in the ground. God plants mustard seed–sized faith inside
each of us. In times of trouble, our faith may seem so small
we no longer think it exists. Ask God to grow your faith big
and strong.

Father, even when trouble comes and I feel
separated from You, You nourish and strengthen
the roots of my faith. Thank You, Father. Amen.

Night 294
WHAT'S FAIR?

"Eye for eye, tooth for tooth,
hand for hand, foot for foot."
EXODUS 21:24

Some verses in the Bible seem cruel, like this one from the book of Exodus. But these words are really about fairness in judgment. God told the people of Israel that when two fighters came before the court, a judge was to order a punishment that fit the crime. If the victim lost an eye in a fight, for example, the judge was not to order that the other guy be put to death. Judges today follow similar laws so the punishment a person receives is fair for the crime that was committed. God wants us to be fair too. He holds us to an even higher standard. When someone hurts us, we are to forgive that person and allow God to be the judge.

God, give me grace to forgive my enemies. I have
been hurt by others, but so was Jesus, and He
readily forgave! Help me to be more like Him. Amen.

STUBBORN HEARTS

Their minds are in darkness. They are strangers to the life of God. This is because they have closed their minds to Him and have turned their hearts away from Him.

EPHESIANS 4:18

Has stubbornness ever kept you from doing something you really wanted to do? Maybe you felt awkward, afraid, or unwanted, so you said, "I don't want to go," or "I don't care." Some people are just as stubborn about not accepting Jesus into their hearts. The consequences of that are far worse than missing out on a good time. Hardening their hearts to Jesus could mean that those people will never get to heaven. Do you know people who refuse to accept Jesus? Then pray every day that they will give up their stubbornness. Ask God to show you if there's something else you can do to help lead them to Christ.

Lord, I reach out to You in prayer asking You to soften the hearts of those too stubborn to come to You themselves. Open their hearts to receive You, Lord. Amen.

Night 296
GOD LIGHTS THE WAY

He makes the winds carry His news.
He makes His helpers a burning fire.

PSALM 104:4

✴

In Hebrews 1:7 Paul explains, "[God] said this about the angels, 'He makes His angels to be winds.' " Then he continues in Hebrews 1:14 telling us that angels are spirits who work for God to help save us from sin. The second part of Psalm 104:4 can be explained through one of the references to fire in the Bible: God became a pillar of fire that led the Israelites out of Egypt (Exodus 13:21–22). God was in the fire, commanding it to go on ahead and light the way for the Israelites when they traveled by night. God sends His angels all over the earth to help us stay away from sin, and He is in control of everything. He goes ahead of us, lighting the way.

Angels are proof that You love us and want to protect us. Thank You, Father, for sending Your angels. Thank You for Your love. Amen.

Night 297
A GRATEFUL HEART

Whatever work you do, do it with all your
heart. Do it for the Lord and not for men.

COLOSSIANS 3:23

There are times, like when we're watching a beautiful sunset
or having a fun time with our friends, when we think about
God's gifts to us. Most of the time, though, we are busy with
everyday tasks, and our minds are far from God. We need to
remember that those everyday tasks are His gifts to us too.
The only difference is in how grateful we are. It's easy to think
you are working for the Lord when you are helping others
or doing something important. But it's much more difficult
when you are taking out the trash or doing homework. Get
into the habit of thanking God for whatever work you do.

Jesus, everything You did, You did for God
and for me. You never complained or refused
to do something. I want to be like You—ready
and willing whatever the task. Amen.

Night 298
WHAT WE NEED

For as he thinks in his heart, so is he. He says to you, "Eat and drink!" But his heart is not with you.

PROVERBS 23:7

✳

Getting what we want is not about having faith that God can do it for us. It is more about having faith that God will give us what He knows we *need*, what is *best* for us. Imagine a kid wishing for a castle to play in. God wouldn't make a castle appear mysteriously in the backyard, but He might put the thought in a dad's head to build a tree house, which ends up being much more fun than a castle anyway. When you pray and ask God for something, know that you might not get what you ask for. Have faith, though, that He will *always* give you what you need. You can count on it.

God, thank You for Your gifts. Teach me not only to have faith in Your generosity but also to be worthy and accepting of whatever You choose to give me. Amen.

Night 299
PERFECTLY WISE AND RIGHT

"Heaven and earth will pass away,
but My Words will not pass away."

MARK 13:31

✳

As humans, we change our minds as we go through our lives. As kids grow up, they change the way they think. With their minds constantly learning new information, they can make better choices with how they feel about things. That's not how it works with God, though. He didn't start out like a child having to learn. God has been perfectly wise and right forever. And because of His perfect wisdom, His Word will never change. We can be sure, as Mark 13:31 shows us, that what God says will still be true tomorrow, next week, next year, and *forever*.

O God, I can always count on Your Word.
What You have said is the truth and the same
today as it will be forever. I trust in You,
Father. Your wisdom never fails. Amen.

Night 300
BE READY WITH GOD'S TRUTH

"The men of God say things that are not true, and the religious leaders rule by their own thoughts. And My people love to have it this way! But what will you do in the end?"

JEREMIAH 5:31

What exactly is a false prophet? It's someone who will try to tell you things about God that just aren't true. It's important that you learn to spot a false prophet when you see one. The Word of God is your handbook. All of God's rules and His best advice are found in the scriptures. The more you know about what is in the Bible, the easier it will be to know when someone is lying to you about God. You should also pray. Ask God to help you spot false teachers and not allow any of their words to seep into your mind and heart. Don't try to stand up to those false prophets alone. Arm yourself with the Bible and be ready to answer with God's truth.

Lord, I don't want to be tricked by people spreading lies about You. I want to be true to Your perfect Word. Amen.

Night 301
WHEN GOD LOOKS AT YOU

*Anyone who hears the Word of God and does
not obey is like a man looking at his face
in a mirror. After he sees himself and goes
away, he forgets what he looks like.*

JAMES 1:23–24

Imagine there was a mirror that showed your true nature—the kind of person you really are inside. Would you want to look? What would you expect to see? James tells us there is such a mirror. It's the Bible. When we know what's in it, we can compare what we look like inside with the way God wants us to be. The Bible does more than show us our faults; it shows us the way God created us to be. When we walk away from the mirror, we need to remember the image of how God made us. When God looks at you, He sees the wonderful human He created. God always looks at you with love, and He wants to see you living your life trying to be like Jesus.

* * *

*Dear God, when I look in the mirror, I want to
see Jesus. Help me to be a reflection of the life
He lived and the things that He taught. Amen.*

Night 302
THE MOST IMPORTANT CHOICE

"See, I have put in front of you today life and what is good, and death and what is bad."

DEUTERONOMY 30:15

✳

Choices. We face them every day. Some are easy. Some are hard. Choices can be unimportant. Or important. Tonight's verse is about the most important choice of all: choosing between God and Satan. Moses is speaking to the Israelites. He's telling them that choosing God leads to a good life, but choosing Satan leads only to what is bad. The Israelites listened halfheartedly to Moses, and because of that, they allowed Satan to trap them into doing what they knew was wrong. Listen to Moses' words in Deuteronomy 30:15. Memorize this verse so you can remember the words when you need to choose between right and wrong. Then, choose wisely.

Lord, bless me with the wisdom to choose the right way. Help me to follow the path that leads away from Satan and brings me to You. Amen.

Night 303
GIFTS OF LOVE

God does not change His mind when He chooses men and gives them His gifts.

ROMANS 11:29

✴

Many holidays include gift giving, and much thought goes into choosing a gift the receiver will like. You might even change your mind a few times about which gift to choose. God is not like humans when He gives gifts. He doesn't need a special occasion. He blesses us with His gifts every day for no other reason than He loves us. God always knows what we need, so we'll never have to return His gifts. And He won't ever take a gift back because He thinks we don't deserve it. God's gifts are all around you: family, friends, pets. . .how many more can you name? Thank Him for His gifts. Use them wisely. And remember to share them whenever you can.

Father, thank You for all those "just because" gifts—priceless one-of-a-kind gifts just because You love me. Help me to take good care of them and use them to please You. Amen.

Night 304
GOD SENDS HELP

"I will have shepherds over them who will care for them. And they will not be afraid any longer, or filled with fear, and none of them will be missing," says the Lord.

JEREMIAH 23:4

We can't know why God allowed a tragedy to take place, but we can be sure that He sends help when it happens. Jeremiah 23:4 shows us how God often works in the world—He works through people. Repeatedly in the Old and New Testaments we find God using people to reach out to a hurting world. And God still works through people today. When a disaster strikes, He sends help through churches, hospitals, food pantries, disaster-relief workers, and a crowd of other volunteers who help in many ways. You can be sure that if disaster strikes, God's helpers will show up right away. They always have, and they always will!

God, every day I see You working through good people in the world. I want to volunteer! How can I help? Amen.

But you, man of God, turn away from all
these sinful things. Work at being right with
God. Live a God-like life. Have faith and love.
Be willing to wait. Have a kind heart.

1 TIMOTHY 6:11

Paul loved his young friend Timothy as though he were his son. Paul wanted to help Timothy succeed, so Paul wrote him two letters full of advice. "I write to you, Timothy. You are my son in the Christian faith. May God the Father and Jesus Christ our Lord give you His loving-favor and loving-kindness and peace" (1 Timothy 1:2). That is how Paul began his first letter. Then he went on giving Timothy advice: "Turn away from all these sinful things," Paul wrote. "Work at being right with God. Live a God-like life. Have faith and love. Be willing to wait. Have a kind heart." Paul's advice is good for all of us! Do your best to follow it, and you will surely please God.

Dear Father, help me, please, to follow
Paul's advice. I want to serve You well. Amen.

Night 306
ASK GOD TO LEAD YOU

This is what the Lord says to Cyrus. . ."I send
him to put nations under his power, and to take
away the power of kings. And I will open doors
in front of him so that gates will not be shut."

ISAIAH 45:1

Will you be married in twenty years? Will you have kids?
God knows. He has *always* known. In the Bible, God tells His
prophets in advance what will happen many years into the
future. These words from Isaiah are an example. Through
the prophet Isaiah, God tells Cyrus why He made him a king
and what will happen to him in the future. We can believe
that what the prophets said in the Bible is the absolute truth
given by God. But we must be very careful about people
today who say that they know the future. Always turn to the
Bible to help you with decisions about your future. Pray and
ask God to lead you where He wants you to go.

Heavenly Father, I know that I can always
trust Your answers to my prayers and the
truthfulness of Your Word. Amen.

LOVE INSTEAD OF JUDGE

Only God can say what is right or wrong.
He made the Law. He can save or put to death.
How can we say if our brother is right or wrong?

JAMES 4:12

Have you ever "gotten even" with someone over something?
Have you ever reacted unkindly to someone else's unkind-
ness? We've all done it. This is what we think they deserve,
so we give it to them. Does that kind of judgment make us
better people? No, never! So, what should we do instead?
We should love others like the Bible tells us to. Jesus taught
us to love God and one another. It's the answer to every
problem. It's the way Jesus lived when He was on earth.
Judging others usually only makes us deserve a harsh judgment in return. Don't judge. . .love. And keep this in mind:
God loves us even when we aren't so loving toward Him!

Jesus, I am no better than anyone else, so who am
I to judge others? Help me, Jesus. Help me not to
judge them but to love them instead. Amen.

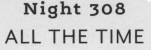

Night 308
ALL THE TIME

I praise You seven times a day,
because Your Law is right.

PSALM 119:164

King David prayed seven times a day. He lifted up praises to God throughout the entire day, every day. He filled the minutes of his life with thankfulness and paying attention to God. The Bible tells us to pray all the time. But how is that possible? You can set up times during your day to pray. Say a prayer when you get up in the morning and before you go to bed. Pray before each meal. You can pray just before you start your homework or before a sports event. Write down a prayer schedule for tomorrow so you pray at least seven times. Use it to help you get into the habit of praying little prayers throughout the day.

God, sometimes I forget to pray. But I can change that! I will set times throughout my day to pray and praise You. Amen.

Night 309
TALK ABOUT IT

*Tell your sins to each other. And pray for
each other so you may be healed.*

JAMES 5:16

✳

James, the author of tonight's verse, says that you should
share your problems with others. If your problem is because
you have done something wrong, that shouldn't keep you
from talking about it. When you share your sins with others,
they can pray for you, help you to feel better about yourself,
and lead you to do better next time. Be careful whom you
choose to share with. It should be someone who knows and
loves Jesus like you do. A family member is best, or a trusted
friend. And don't ever be afraid to talk with God about your
sins. He already knows if you have done something wrong,
and He is ready to forgive you. You are His child, and He
loves you!

Heavenly Father, there are things that I am
keeping to myself that bother me. Help me
to share them with the right Christian family
member or friend. Lead me, Lord. Amen.

Joshua said, "So put away the strange
gods that are among you. Give your
hearts to the Lord, the God of Israel."

JOSHUA 24:23

The Israelites knew that God performed many miracles,
like dividing the Red Sea, providing food for them in the
wilderness, and destroying Jericho's walls with blasts from
a few trumpets. You would think their faith in God would
be strong. But many Israelites worshipped false gods—
or idols—as they wandered through the desert looking for
the Promised Land. Joshua saw and was troubled by all the
false-god worship. He told his friends to stop it and then
ordered them to show God their faith in Him by destroying
their idols. The Israelites listened and threw away their false
gods. Think about it: Is anything getting in the way of your
relationship with God?

Dear God, make clear to me the things in this
world that have become my idols. You are my
God, and I choose to serve only You. Amen.

Night 311
FAITHFUL

He said to the Jews who believed, "If you keep and obey My Word, then you are My followers for sure."

JOHN 8:31

✳

Jesus taught us how to live in two ways. His wise words made clear what God expected of us. But more importantly, Jesus taught by example. Jesus wants us to live like He did, doing what God expects of us. . .not just on Sunday when we worship Him in church, but every day. Jesus said that we are truly His followers if we are faithful. This means we act like Christians every day, all day long. Faithfulness also means trusting God to forgive us when we mess up and do something wrong. Remember: Jesus is faithful to you all the time, so do your best to be faithful to Him.

Jesus, Your faithfulness to me is so great. You've set the perfect example for living, and You are so patient with me while I try to be like You. Thank You, Jesus. Amen.

Night 312
MORE THAN FAIR

Punish me when I need it, O Lord,
but be fair. Do not punish me in Your anger,
or You will bring me to nothing.

JEREMIAH 10:24

Jeremiah was upset with himself because, as hard as he tried to obey God, he still messed up. He knew that God had every right to be angry with him for his sins. If God gave Jeremiah the punishment he knew he deserved, Jeremiah would have nothing left. In the first part of the verse, Jeremiah begs God to be fair with His punishment. But God is *always* fair! He sent His Son, Jesus, to take all the punishment that Jeremiah and everyone else deserved for their sins, and not just in Bible times, but forever. When we believe this, God will forgive us, and we don't have to worry about His anger. Now that's *more* than fair!

Dear God, thank You for always being fair with me. I know that when I confess my sins to You, You will be gentle and loving toward me and say, "I forgive you." I love You, God. Amen.

Night 313
ALL AROUND US

Jesus said to him, "Thomas, because you have seen Me, you believe. Those are happy who have never seen Me and yet believe!"

JOHN 20:29

Soon after Jesus rose from the grave, He appeared to some of His disciples. One of them, Thomas, had not been part of those first Jesus sightings. When others told him they had seen Jesus, he refused to believe—he wanted proof that Jesus was alive. One week later, Thomas got his proof when Jesus walked through the locked doors of a room where the disciples were staying. He invited Thomas to feel where the nails had been in His hands and to touch His side that had been stabbed with a sword. Jesus mildly scolded Thomas, saying, "Do not doubt, believe!" (John 20:27). Jesus does appear to us—through His words in the Bible and His Spirit that lives in us every day.

Dear Jesus, You are all around me. I see You in the sun, the moon, the stars, and many other ways. Amen.

Night 314
GOD'S SENSE OF HUMOR

He Who sits in the heavens laughs.
The Lord makes fun of them.

PSALM 2:4

God definitely has a sense of humor. After all, He made us in His image, and *we* laugh. Psalm 2:4 in the Bible says it clearly: "He Who sits in the heavens laughs." And you know that everything in the Bible is true. But what's that about God making fun of people? Imagine God looking down at us. He sees people trying to hide from Him, or at least trying to hide their sins from Him. Everywhere God looks, people think they can outsmart Him. No one can outsmart God or change His plans for our lives. So God sits up there in heaven looking down at all of the ridiculous things people say and do. "Those silly people!" He says. And He laughs.

• •

O God, how foolish we humans are! I'm glad
that You can look at us with a sense of humor.
No one can outsmart You, ever. Amen.

COURAGE TO KEEP GOING

We are pressed on every side, but we still have room to move. We are often in much trouble, but we never give up. People make it hard for us, but we are not left alone. We are knocked down, but we are not destroyed.

2 CORINTHIANS 4:8–9

If you think about it, God uses His power to make us into mini superheroes. Imagine yourself trapped in a situation where there seems to be no way out. What does God do? He provides some wiggle room so you can escape by following His commands. When you feel like you've done all you can, God gives you courage to keep going. The enemy might make it hard for you, but God is always by your side, helping you to fight. You might get knocked down a few times, but you will never be destroyed, because God promises you eternal life! God is great, and He uses His greatness to work through us. Nothing can overpower us when we put all our faith in Him.

Heavenly Father, thank You for using Your power to help me overcome any trouble in my life. Amen.

Night 316
HEADED IN THE RIGHT DIRECTION

You do not know about tomorrow. What is your life? It is like fog. You see it and soon it is gone.

JAMES 4:14

For thirty-five years, a man named Arthur Stace wrote the word *eternity* in chalk across Sydney, Australia. He had been a criminal before finding faith in Jesus and turning his life around. His word writing was an attempt to get people thinking about where they were headed—not only in this life but also in the next. And in this Bible verse, James wants us to think about where we're headed. Without Jesus in our lives, we walk around as if in a fog. We don't know what tomorrow will bring. But putting our faith in Jesus *every* day means we are headed in the right direction—toward forever life in heaven with Him—never-ending tomorrows!

Jesus, I feel joyful knowing that I will spend eternity with You. Thank You for coming into my heart and guiding me every day. Amen.

LEARNING THE BIBLE

So David. . .ruled over all Israel. And he ruled over
Israel for forty years. . . . Then he died as an old
man. . . . And his son Solomon ruled in his place.
The acts of King David. . .are written in the books
of Samuel, Nathan, and Gad, the men of God.

1 CHRONICLES 29:26–29

✳

This Bible passage helps us to understand a little more about
King David. As king, David ruled over Israel for forty years.
When he died, Solomon became the new king. Solomon is
known for his wisdom; many of his wise sayings are found in
the book of Proverbs. Much of what we know about David
came from Samuel, Nathan, and Gad. Samuel is a well-known
Old Testament prophet, but Nathan and Gad are not. Some
Bible teachers believe that their "books" are part of the books
of First and Second Samuel in the Bible. Ask your parents
to allow you to search for David's name in an online Bible.
See what you can find out about this great king.

God, I want to learn more about the people
in the Bible. Teach me, Lord. Amen.

Night 318
WHEN YOU'RE AFRAID. . .

When we arrived in the country of Macedonia,
we had no rest. We had all kinds of trouble. There
was fighting all around us. Our hearts were afraid.

2 CORINTHIANS 7:5

God's people have always faced situations where they felt afraid. For example, 2 Corinthians 7:5 tells us that Paul and his friends felt afraid after arriving in the country of Macedonia. They had gone there to preach the gospel, but they were tired. There was all kinds of trouble and fighting around them, and they were scared. Often when we are afraid, God sends someone to help. And that's exactly what He did for Paul and his companions. God sent Paul's friend Titus to comfort them. Just seeing and talking with Titus made Paul feel happy (vv. 6–7). God understands when you are afraid, and He will help you. You can count on it!

Father, is there someone I know who is worried
or afraid? Please teach me how I might comfort
them and bring them some happiness. Amen.

Night 319
KEEP RUNNING!

All these many people who have had faith in God are around us like a cloud. Let us put every thing out of our lives that keeps us from doing what we should. Let us keep running in the race that God has planned for us.

HEBREWS 12:1

Being a Christian is sort of like running a marathon, a race in which heaven is our goal. As we race through life, other Christians cheer us on. They encourage us to get past anything that gets in our way and keeps us from finishing. Our Christian friends surround us like a great cloud as they help us run toward Jesus. Don't give up. Keep running! Someday you will reach the finish line—heaven—and God Himself will be there cheering you on.

This race through life is hard, but I will stay strong and give it my best effort. If I fall, Lord, lift me up. If I become weak, carry me. We'll cross the finish line together. Amen.

Night 320
DO YOU TRUST GOD?

"Do not be afraid of them or of what they say, even if thistles and thorns are with you and you sit on scorpions."

 EZEKIEL 2:6

Don't be afraid—"even if thistles and thorns are with you and you sit on scorpions." *Ouch!* If anyone else but God had said it, the prophet Ezekiel probably would have answered, "How can I *not* be afraid?" But Ezekiel trusted God, and he did what God wanted. He went to tell the Israelites to shape up and stop sinning—even though he knew the people would want to kill him! What if God asked you to step out of your comfort zone and do something that you were afraid to do? Would you trust God and do it? New people, places, and things can be scary. But God will be with you all the way. So don't be afraid.

Dear Lord, remove my fear so that I can boldly follow Your plan for my life. And encourage me never to be afraid to tell others about Jesus. Amen.

STAND UP TO TROUBLE

Watch and keep awake! Stand true to the Lord.
Keep on acting like men and be strong.

1 CORINTHIANS 16:13

✴

These words are from Paul's letter to his church friends in Corinth. "Watch and keep awake! Stand true to the Lord." Paul's words create an image of God's army facing its enemy. Instead of running, the army stands and fights. Paul's friends were facing a difficult time for their Christian beliefs. People hated them for loving Jesus. So, Paul, through his word picture, told them to be on the lookout for trouble, to stand up to trouble instead of running, and to be brave and strong. That's how all Christians should be when trouble comes to steal their faith. How about you? Are you a soldier in God's army?

Dear God, help me to be ready when trouble comes. Bless me with courage. Strengthen my faith so that I can stand up and fight for what's right and true. Amen.

Night 322
STRENGTH-BOOSTER

*He gives strength to the weak. And He gives
power to him who has little strength.*

ISAIAH 40:29

✳

The Bible is filled with God's promises, and today's verse is one of them. God says that when we think we aren't strong enough to accomplish what He has planned for us, He will boost our strength. To tap into God's strength-booster, we need faith. We need to believe in God's promises and trust Him. Prayer is important too. When we face something difficult, we should pray and ask God to help us. And He will. How can we be sure? Because He promised! And God cannot lie. The Bible says so (Numbers 23:19)!

• •

*Father God, it makes me feel good to know
that whatever kind of strength I need, You will
certainly give it to me. Thank You, Father. Amen.*

Night 323
SONGS OF PRAISE

Tell of your joy to each other by singing the Songs of
David and church songs. Sing in your heart to the Lord.

EPHESIANS 5:19

✳

Rewind your thoughts to a different time two thousand years
ago. Electricity was limited to lightning in the night sky. There
were no cell towers or anything else to carry sound from
one place to another. Music consisted of simple musical
instruments and the human voice. In this quiet setting, Paul
wrote to his friends in Ephesus and suggested that making
music together is a good way to connect with God. He told
them to sing the psalms that David wrote, to sing joyfully,
and to put heartfelt emotions into their singing. Step away
from the loudness of your world and create your own times
of silence. Then sing your own songs of praise to the Lord.

. . . .

Thank You, Father, for the gift of music.
Let me remember to use it often to connect
with You in praise and in song. Amen.

Night 324
POWERFUL VOICE

The voice of the Lord is powerful.
The voice of the Lord is great.

PSALM 29:4

✳

In Bible times, the people of Jericho might have thought the sound of trumpets was the loudest sound they had ever heard—a sound loud enough to bring down the city walls! Daniel might have answered that a lion's roar was the loudest sound he had ever heard—just before he was thrown into the lion's den. For the Israelites fleeing Egypt, the loudest sound was probably the thundering hooves of horses pulling chariots filled with enemy soldiers. God's voice is more powerful than any sound anyone has ever heard. In fact, the Bible says His voice is so powerful that it shakes the desert and breaks trees into pieces! Read more about it in Psalm 29:3–9.

O God, You are so powerful that if You speak,
the sound of Your voice shakes the earth!
How great and mighty You are! Amen.

Night 325
WHAT'S YOUR TALENT?

God has given each of you a gift. Use it to help
each other. This will show God's loving-favor.

1 PETER 4:10

✳

Our talents are gifts from God, and everyone has them. They
are, simply put, things that we are good at. This verse tells
us that God gives us these gifts so we can use them to help
others.

Maybe you are really good at reading. Then use that
talent to read to your younger brothers or sisters. Are you
good at drawing? You might make some cards to take to
people in a nursing home. Are you good at cheering people
up? Then get out there and be cheerful! Take a few minutes
to think about your talent—can you think of more than one?
Now get creative and think of ways to use your talents to
help others.

Father, when I share my talents with others,
it's like I'm spreading Your love around! Thank
You for giving me things that I'm good at. Amen.

Night 326
EVEN MORE TALENTS

"You have done well. You are a good and faithful servant. You have been faithful over a few things. I will put many things in your care."
MATTHEW 25:23

Jesus told a story about three servants. Before their master went on a trip, he put his servants in charge of his money. He gave one man five coins, another two coins, and the third received one coin. The servant who had five coins went out and traded until he made five more. The servant who had two coins did the same. He made two more. The servant who had the one coin went and hid it in a hole in the ground. When their master returned, he praised the two servants who had doubled his money. Are you using God's gifts—your talents—or have you hidden them away? Use your gifts to help others, and God will bless you with even more talents!

God, You have given me special gifts to put to use for You. Help me to use them wisely so I can do even more to serve You. Amen.

Night 327
RULES FOR REASONS

Punish your son when he does wrong and he will
give you comfort. Yes, he will give joy to your soul.

PROVERBS 29:17

✳

Laws are in place for a purpose, and breaking them leads
to consequences—in other words, punishment. Rules are
made for reasons, and when kids break their parents' rules,
there are consequences. Proverbs 29:17 is about respect.
It's comforting for parents to see their sons and daughters
learning to obey rules and become respectful adults. It
brings joy to their souls! Try your very best to obey your
parents' rules and God's rules. If you mess up and have
some privileges taken away, accept the punishment willingly. When your parents—and God—see you doing what is
right, it will fill them with joy.

Heavenly Father, I do my best to obey my
parents, but I slip up sometimes and don't
follow their rules. Help me to try harder, God.
I want to please them and You. Amen.

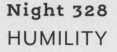

Night 328
HUMILITY

In the same way, you who are younger, submit
yourselves to your elders. All of you, clothe yourselves
with humility toward one another, because, "God
opposes the proud but shows favor to the humble."

1 PETER 5:5 NIV

We can all find someone older and wiser to learn from.
But sometimes we become know-it-alls and decide that
we know more than our elders. Our pride gets in the way
of our learning.

Older kids, parents, grandparents, teachers—you can
learn something from all of them. *Humility* is a word that
means "setting pride aside." When you admit that there is
something you don't know and you are open to someone
teaching you, that's humility. Jesus is a good example of
humility, and God wants you to learn from Him. Practice
humility and see what God does in your life.

Father, open my heart to wisdom offered by those older
than me. Set their wise words inside my heart. Amen.

Night 329
SAY, "THANK YOU!"

There is nothing better for a man than to
eat and drink and find joy in his work. I have
seen that this also is from the hand of God.

ECCLESIASTES 2:24

God's little blessings are all around and even inside you.
Many are blessings you never even notice: The sun rises and
sets every day. Gravity holds you down on earth. You wake
up. You go to sleep. Your heart beats. Lungs push air in and
out. You see, hear, taste, touch, and smell things! When
was the last time you thought of those things as blessings?
Ecclesiastes 2:24 encourages us to remember that all good
things—even the smallest ones—are gifted to us as blessings
from God. Look around. What other simple things do you
see that you haven't thought of as blessings? Remember to
tell God, "Thank You!"

Dear God, open my eyes to the simple things in life,
the things that I forget to notice. You have done so
many wonderful things in and around me. Help me to
enjoy them more thankfully. I'm grateful, Lord. Amen.

Night 330
WHITE AS SNOW

"Come now, let us think about this together,"
says the Lord. "Even though your sins are bright
red, they will be as white as snow. Even though
they are dark red, they will be like wool."

ISAIAH 1:18

✳

Colors have meanings. For example, a traffic signal has a green light that means go, a yellow light that means caution, and a red light that means stop. In Isaiah 1:18, God describes our sins as bright red and dark red. But He says they will be white as snow. White is a color connected with something that is pure and clean. When God sent Jesus to save us, He took the sin out of our hearts and turned all that red stuff to freshly washed white! No need for emergency vehicles with red flashing lights to come to our rescue. Jesus has already saved us!

I will confess my sins to You, God. I praise You for Your forgiveness. How wonderful You are to forgive even my worst sins and give me a clean heart. Amen.

OTHERS WILL NOTICE

But Ruth said, "Do not beg me to leave you
or turn away from following you. I will go
where you go. . . . Your people will be my
people. And your God will be my God."

RUTH 1:16

Elimelech, his wife Naomi, and their two sons moved to a
place called Moab. While there, the sons married women
named Orpah and Ruth. Sadness came when Elimelech and
both sons died, leaving the women alone. Naomi decided
to return home to Israel, and Orpah and Ruth went along.
On the way, Naomi told the girls to go back home (Ruth
1:8). But Ruth wanted to stay with her mother-in-law and
worship Naomi's God—the only God. Maybe it was because
Ruth wanted a faith like Naomi's so she would be strong
and not feel so alone. Trust God during your not-so-good
times, and maybe others will notice, like Ruth did.

Father, I learn a lot about faith from Bible people
like Naomi. Help me to have a strong faith like
hers—faith that others will notice. Amen.

STUFF AND MONEY

The love of money is the beginning of all kinds of sin. Some people have turned from the faith because of their love for money. They have made much pain for themselves because of this.

1 TIMOTHY 6:10

You can just as well substitute the word *stuff* for *money* in this verse, and it will mean the same thing. Paul is telling his friend Timothy that loving money or other possessions too much allows sin to creep in. Paul's warning to Timothy, almost two thousand years ago, is just as fresh today. Loving our stuff too much pulls us away from God. And when that happens, we are more likely to sin, and sin leads to us feeling unhappy. Look around your room. As your eyes set on each thing, take a moment to thank God for it.

Dear Lord, sometimes I pray asking You for more stuff. Teach me to be right with those prayers and to thank You for everything I have. Amen.

Night 333

PEACE NEVER COMES FROM SIN

"They have healed the hurt of My people only a little, saying, 'Peace, peace,' when there is no peace."

JEREMIAH 6:14

Jeremiah had warned the Israelites that God said to shape up and stop worshipping idols. But they kept doing it. Trouble brewed all around them. God was angry. Still, the leaders stood up and said, "Don't worry. Everything is fine." Jeremiah knew that everything was *not* fine! The Israelites believed the lies. But peace never comes from sin. They kept on sinning—and trouble came! When the Holy Spirit whispers in your heart, "Stop doing what you're doing," listen. Don't obey Satan's voice when he tells you, "It's okay. Go on. Everything's going to be fine."

God, please don't allow me to fall into Satan's sinful traps. When he says, "Go on, sin," let me obey Your voice telling me to stop. Amen.

MISSIONARIES

*Dear friend, you are doing a good work by being kind
to the Christians, and for sure, to the strangers.*
3 JOHN 1:5

✳

Today's Bible verse speaks to missionaries serving strangers
in faraway lands. Maybe you would like to be a missionary
someday. That would be great! But a missionary's work is
hard. You could live in a tent among strangers. Often, you
won't have what you need, not even simple things like running
water or a stove. Your job is to teach others about Jesus and,
hopefully, to make them fellow Christians. But some might
hate you and want to hurt you. You could be the only one
showing kindness. You might wonder, sometimes, if being
a missionary is worth it. It *is* worth it. Ask God to lead you
where He wants you to go. Ask Him to use you to show
kindness to others.

Lord, I pray for missionaries serving in the most
dangerous parts of the world. Protect them! God, how
can I serve You through acts of kindness? Amen.

Night 335
CARING FOR EARTH

"While the earth lasts, planting time and gathering time, cold and heat, summer and winter, and day and night will not end."

GENESIS 8:22

This passage comes at the end of Noah's story in the Bible (Genesis 6:9–8:22). After the great flood was over, God invited the ark family to come out. God promised never again to destroy His creatures in an earth-covering flood. As a pledge of His faithfulness, the Creator promises to keep the world spinning on its axis, allowing His cycles and beauty of nature to continue, until the end. Read Genesis 1, and you'll see that God created Adam and Eve to care for His earth. You are today's Adam or Eve. It's your responsibility, as best as you can, to care for His creation. Think about it: What can you do to help care for earth?

Heavenly Father, thank You for the earth! Help me to respect and care for Your creation. Amen.

Night 336
WHO NEEDS JESUS?

All things can be seen when they are in the light.
Everything that can be seen is in the light.

EPHESIANS 5:13

✳

In Ephesians 5:13, the author, Paul, is speaking about living without Jesus in your heart. When your heart is without Him, it's like you are walking around in total darkness bumping into sin all the time. Sin keeps knocking you down until you shout, "Somebody, turn on the light!" To get rid of spiritual darkness, a person needs to ask Jesus into their heart. When a person accepts Jesus as their Savior, it's like warm, bright sunlight floods their heart. Jesus said, "I am the Light of the world. Anyone who follows Me. . .will have the Light of Life" (John 8:12). Do you know someone who needs Jesus to light up their heart? Pray now for that person to accept Jesus.

Dear Jesus, I want _____ to accept You as Savior.
Please, Jesus, light up their heart. Amen.

Night 337

JESUS, GOD, AND THE HOLY SPIRIT

"Hear, O Israel! The Lord our God is one Lord!"
DEUTERONOMY 6:4

God's first two commands are "Have no gods other than Me. Do not make for yourselves a god to look like anything that is in heaven above or on the earth below or in the waters under the earth" (Exodus 20:3–4). But the Israelites didn't obey. Again and again, God's prophets told them to stop it (Deuteronomy 6:4). God then sent Jesus and the Holy Spirit. Some people think of Jesus, God, and the Holy Spirit as three separate beings. But Jesus and the Holy Spirit are part of God. It's hard for us to understand because we humans exist as only one person. God exists as three persons! It is just one of the amazing things about Him that make Him God!

Father God, I can't completely understand how You are three persons all at once, but I do know that You are my one and only God! Amen.

O man, He has told you what is good. What does the
Lord ask of you but to do what is fair and to love
kindness, and to walk without pride with your God?

MICAH 6:8

Kings and queens in stories and in real life are not perfect.
Sin is everywhere. Kingdoms rise and fall. But there is a sin-
free land ruled by a perfect King. . .*heaven*! God's kingdom
is forever. It will never end. God rules both heaven and
earth. Because He is the only good and true King, we should
serve Him well, doing our best to be fair, kind, and loving
toward one another. Always, we should honor our King
with worship and praise. He is the only one worthy of such
things.

O God, my King. How great You are! You lead perfectly,
rule justly, and teach wisely. I am so blessed to be
Your child and to live in Your kingdom forever. Amen.

Night 339
A LITTLE FAITH

At once the father cried out. He said
with tears in his eyes, "Lord, I have faith.
Help my weak faith to be stronger!"

MARK 9:24

Mark 9:14–29 tells of a father who brings his son to the disciples asking them to cast out an evil spirit. The man's words "If You can do anything" (v.22) show that the man did not have complete faith in Jesus. So why did Jesus still heal the boy? The answer might be in the father's words "Lord, I have faith. Help my weak faith to be stronger!" Sometimes, a little faith is enough. Jesus says that even a little faith can accomplish great things (Matthew 17:20; Luke 17:6). When you only have a little faith, you can pray to God to strengthen your faith and make it bigger. Only then can God truly begin to work through you.

Dear Lord, there are days when my faith is strong and others when I slip into doubt. Please keep my doubt from getting bigger. Strengthen my faith, Lord! Amen.

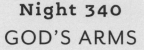

Night 340
GOD'S ARMS

Of what great worth is Your loving-kindness,
O God! The children of men come and are
safe in the shadow of Your wings.

PSALM 36:7

Tonight's scripture verse holds a comforting thought—it paints a picture of a kind and loving God. A God whose children know that whenever they feel afraid, they can run to Him. He will cover them with protection the way a mother bird protects her babies with her wings. God loves you more than you can ever imagine, and He will never leave you alone and unprotected. His loving-kindness is all around you all the time. You never have to feel afraid with God as your Father. But you are human, and all humans feel fear. So whenever you feel frightened, remember this: God has His arms around you. He will hold you tight and keep you safe.

Thank You, Father, for Your loving protection.
I know that I am always safe with You
holding me in Your arms. Amen.

Night 341
IN YOUR HEART

> "It will not be said, 'See, here it is!' or,
> 'There it is!' For the holy nation of God is in you."
>
> LUKE 17:21

✳

For centuries, the Jewish people waited for God's kingdom to arrive. The words of the prophets were not about some new kingdom on earth with a new king but instead about the kingdom of heaven and God, our Great King. As Christians, we know that God's kingdom exists in our hearts. If we've discovered the kingdom, it means that God (our King) has saved us from sin through His Son, Jesus. It's like God sits on a throne in our very own hearts, ruling our souls and thoughts. God promises to live within us until that day when we are free from our bodies and our souls go to be with Him in heaven. Isn't that awesome?

• •

Dear Father, Your kingdom is within me—
in my heart. I look forward to when I will
live with You forever in heaven. Amen.

Night 342
BE HAPPY FOR OTHERS

Then Saul became very angry. . . . He said,
"They have given David honor for ten thousands,
but for me only thousands. Now what more can
he have but to be king?" And Saul was jealous
and did not trust David from that day on.

1 SAMUEL 18:8–9

✳

King Saul was a powerful king who fought his enemies and
won (1 Samuel 14:47). At the time, David was a smart young
soldier in Saul's army. He was such a successful soldier that
he received higher praises than Saul. And that made the king
jealous and angry. Although David had proved himself loyal
to the king, Saul's jealousy blinded him to the talents and
accomplishments of his faithful subject. As a result, God
removed Saul as king of Israel (1 Samuel 15:26). Jealousy is
a feeling that leads to nothing good. When others succeed,
especially at something we want, God expects us to be gen-
uinely happy for them and cheer them on.

God, help me to overcome jealousy and
to treat others as Jesus would. Amen.

Night 343
LIGHT OF THE HOLY SPIRIT

Do not quench the Spirit.
1 THESSALONIANS 5:19 NIV

✳

Paul compares the Holy Spirit to fire and warns his friends to be careful not to let the fire go out. Paul said his friends should do these things: pray, have a thankful attitude in all circumstances, and believe in God's will for their lives. Also, they were to speak out against laziness, help those who were shy about sharing the gospel, and examine the things they were being taught. They needed to hang on to what was good and stay away from evil. By doing all these things, they wouldn't be putting out the fire of the Holy Spirit. Follow Paul's instructions to his friends. Then you will keep the Spirit burning brightly in your heart.

Lord, help me to keep the warmth and light of
the Holy Spirit burning inside my heart. Amen.

Night 344
WILLING TO SHARE THE TRUTH

But if I say, "I will not remember Him or speak any more in His name," then in my heart it is like a burning fire shut up in my bones. I am tired of holding it in, and I cannot do that.

JEREMIAH 20:9

The prophet Jeremiah had been called by God to warn the people that unless they stopped sinning and asked God to forgive them, trouble would come. Jeremiah preached with all his might, but the people only made fun of him. Frustrated, Jeremiah decided to stay silent. But, no matter how hard he tried, Jeremiah couldn't stop thinking about God's warning. He couldn't stay silent! So, Jeremiah continued preaching the Word of God. God is looking for Christians like Jeremiah who are willing to share the truth of His Word—no matter what. Don't be shy or ashamed of sharing the Good News about Jesus! If people make fun of you, let God be their judge.

Jesus, help me never to stay silent where I can share the Good News. Amen.

Night 345
HOW WOULD YOU DESCRIBE GOD?

And God said to Moses, "I AM WHO I AM."
EXODUS 3:14

Look at yourself in the mirror, then finish this sentence with words that describe how you look. "I am _____." It's easy to describe what you see, but what about something you can't see? How would you describe God? No one knows what God looks like because He doesn't have a physical body like humans. But we can describe things about God's personality. We know that He is perfect, loving, forgiving all-knowing, forever. . . God thinks of us as His children, and we know what He says because He speaks to us through the Bible. And God wants us to be His voice on earth. He wants us to tell the whole world about Him. So do it!

. . . .

Heavenly Father, what an awesome
responsibility to be Your voice in the world!
Help me to speak Your Word. Amen.

Night 346
THE BIBLE WILL LAST FOREVER

These also are wise sayings of Solomon, which were written down by the men of Hezekiah, king of Judah.

PROVERBS 25:1

✳

King Solomon had a way with words. The Bible tells us that he spoke three thousand proverbs—or wise sayings—and he wrote 1,005 songs (1 Kings 4:32)! In ancient times, the Bible was not complete the way we know it today. Scribes— writers—had to write the words on scrolls, and that took time. Some of the scrolls were even lost or misplaced. Thanks to scribes and others, the Word of God was written down and has been passed from generation to generation. We know that the Bible will last forever. Jesus said, "Heaven and earth will pass away, but My words will not pass away" (Matthew 24:35).

• •

Dear God, Your Word will live on forever. Nothing can take it from us. It is Your voice speaking to Your children from generation to generation. Amen.

GOD-PLEASER

I have seen that all the work done is because a
man wants what his neighbor has. This also is
for nothing, like trying to catch the wind.

ECCLESIASTES 4:4

God gave a warning in His Ten Commandments: "Do not
have a desire for your neighbor's house. . .or anything that
belongs to your neighbor" (Exodus 20:17). There is nothing
wrong with following someone's good example. Jesus, for
instance, is our best example. But when we work to be like
other people so we can get all the stuff they have—that's
when it becomes a problem. Solomon says that our work
is for nothing when we try to be like others or get what
they have. God wants everything we work at to bring us closer
to Him. That means reaching out to help those neighbors
and others in need. How can you work for the Lord?

Lord, remind me that my work and all that I
do should be pleasing in Your sight. Amen.

Night 348
GRATEFUL AND GLAD

When He had given thanks, He broke it and said,
"Take this bread and eat it. This is My body which
is broken for you. Do this to remember Me."

1 CORINTHIANS 11:24

Maybe you've heard this Bible verse when communion was offered in your church. The words are Jesus' words to us, asking us to remember His death on the cross. If Jesus hadn't done what He did, there would be no way for us to some-day get into heaven and live forever. We might think, *Wow, I didn't deserve for Him to do that for me!* And it's true—none of us deserved Jesus' gift to us. But He gave it to us anyway. When we remember His death on the cross, we should be thankful; and when we remember that He rose from His grave, we should be glad! His resurrection reminds us that we will have forever life too—with Him in heaven.

Jesus, fill my mind and heart with thoughts of
Your death, burial, and resurrection. I am
so grateful for Your sacrifice. I don't ever
want to take it for granted. Amen.

Night 349
SOMETHING GOOD

*We know that God makes all things work
together for the good of those who love Him
and are chosen to be a part of His plan.*

ROMANS 8:28

Some artists are really good at putting together pieces of junk
to create something beautiful. Old pipes, a bicycle wheel, a
rusty shovel, maybe a tin bucket or two. . .it might look like
junk to us, but the artist has already planned how all those
things can work together to make something good. God,
the Great Creator, is that sort of artist. He takes the junk in
our lives, the bad stuff that happens, and somehow makes
it all into something good! The Creator doesn't just throw
stuff together and call it art. He always has a plan, and His
plan is perfect. When bad stuff happens, trust God to take
it and make it into something good.

*Dear God, take all the bad stuff that has ever
happened and create something good. I can't
wait to see what You will do with it. Amen.*

Night 350
GOD KNOWS BEST

"If you get your life from Me and My Words live in you, ask whatever you want. It will be done for you."

JOHN 15:7

✳

There are people who pray thinking that God will give them everything they ask for. But the Creator won't give us what we want unless it lines up with what He wants us to have. As we pray and ask God for what we want, we need to understand that He knows what is best for us, and we should never demand "our way." Read again the first part of John 15:7 that says, "If you get your life from Me and My Words live in you." This shows that God wants us to put our trust in Him. When you pray, ask God for what you want, but then tell Him that you want Him to give you what's best. He knows how to make that happen.

Father, You know best. I want what You want for me, even if it's not what I ask for. Amen.

Night 351
QUESTIONING GOD

And the Lord said, "Have you
any reason to be angry?"

JONAH 4:4

God told Jonah to go and tell the wicked people of Nineveh that He would soon be passing judgment on them. Instead Jonah ran away and ended up on a boat that he was tossed from in the middle of a raging storm. Jonah didn't drown though; God sent a big fish to swallow him. When Jonah asked for forgiveness, God made the fish spit him out. Jonah then traveled to Nineveh and delivered God's message, and the people asked for forgiveness. God decided not to destroy them. This made Jonah angry! Jonah had forgotten that God is in charge, and His actions are always fair. We have no right to question what He does—even when it makes us angry.

I'm guilty of questioning You, God. I wonder
why You do what You do, and sometimes I
get angry. Forgive me, please. Amen.

Night 352
THE STORY OF JESUS

The missionaries told with much power how Jesus was raised from the dead. God's favor was on them all.

ACTS 4:33

✴

A missionary's most important job is telling others the story of Jesus, especially the good news that Jesus is our way to heaven. Missionaries trust God to lead them wherever they go and to give them His power to preach the good news. Often, missionaries run into trouble in faraway lands. Some have even lost their lives for preaching the good news. If you think about it, that is exactly what happened to Jesus' followers in ancient days. They were turned away, punished, and killed for loving Jesus and sharing His story. But that didn't stop them from sharing the good news. They have kept on working for the Lord to this very day! Pray for missionaries. Ask God to keep them safe and to give them His power when they preach the good news.

* * *

Father, please bring all missionaries to safety wherever they are. Give them the power and strength to do Your work. And, God, help me to work for You too. Amen.

Night 353
POWER OVER THE WORLD

Who could have power over the world except
by believing that Jesus is the Son of God?

1 JOHN 5:5

We Christians do have some power over the world. Our power is different from God's though. For us, the world is a sinful place full of temptation. Almost everywhere we go, we face things that we know are wrong. We need to choose: Do we go the right way or the wrong way? Faith helps us make the right choices. When we welcome Jesus into our hearts, we have faith that He will help us have power over the worldly sins that tempt us. When we listen to Him and make right choices, that is how we have power over a world filled with sin. Can you think of a time when you faced a right or wrong decision? If you made the right choice, you used your faith to have power over the world!

Jesus, I believe in You! Help me to overpower any sin that gets in my way. Amen.

Night 354
NOTHING IS IMPOSSIBLE

"So I bought the field at Anathoth from Hanamel,
the son of my father's brother. And I weighed
out seventeen pieces of silver for him."

JEREMIAH 32:9

Jeremiah warned the Jews that if they didn't shape up, God would send the Babylonians to conquer them. And Jerusalem's rulers threw him in prison because of his warnings. In Jeremiah's lowest moment, his cousin Hanamel showed up. He needed money for food and wanted to sell his field, but it was in the village of Anathoth, where it couldn't do Jeremiah any good. God told Jeremiah to buy it, so he did. And God told Jeremiah that his situation would get much better (Jeremiah 32:36–44). Jeremiah trusted that it would happen—and it did! If you feel trapped by a situation, remember these words that God spoke to Jeremiah: "I am the Lord. . . . Is anything too hard for Me?" (Jeremiah 32:27).

When I face problems, Lord, I know that
You have the answers. Show me the way.
Nothing is impossible for You. Amen.

Night 355
YOUR ARMOR

Wear a belt of truth around your body. Wear a piece of iron over your chest which is being right with God. Wear shoes on your feet which are the Good News of peace. Most important of all, you need a covering of faith in front of you. This is to put out the fire-arrows of the devil. The covering for your head is that you have been saved from the punishment of sin. Take the sword of the Spirit which is the Word of God.

EPHESIANS 6:14–17

In these verses, Paul describes the kind of "armor" (behavior) Christians need to protect themselves from Satan. Paul said that we need to believe the truth about God and be right with Him. We should be ready to share the good news about Jesus wherever our feet take us. Most importantly, we need faith so we don't fall into Satan's traps. We need to remember Jesus' gift of forgiveness for our sins. And, finally, arming ourselves with God's Word helps us fight Satan's lies. How does your armor measure up?

I have put on my armor, God. Amen.

PRIDE

All at once the fingers of a man's hand were seen writing on the wall. . . . Then the king's face turned white, and his thoughts turned to fear. His legs became weak and his knees began shaking.

DANIEL 5:5–6

You've thrown a party for a thousand friends. Everyone is having a good time, when a human hand with no body appears and begins writing graffiti on the wall! That's just what happened at King Belshazzar's banquet. King Belshazzar was so proud of what he'd done—making his kingdom safe—that he threw himself a party. No one could read that creepy message on the wall except a man named Daniel. He read it to the king: "God has numbered the days of your rule and has brought it to an end" (Daniel 5: 26). Soon, God allowed the enemy soldiers to get past the wall and invade the kingdom. What's the message of this real story from the Bible? Great pride can get you into great trouble!

God, please don't let pride take hold of me. You are the one who allows me to do great things. Amen.

DON'T LOSE HOPE

While Jesus spoke, men came from the house of
the leader of the place of worship. They said, "Your
daughter is dead. Why trouble the Teacher anymore?"

MARK 5:35

✳

Jairus asked Jesus to heal his daughter. But while Jairus and
Jesus were on the way, they received news that the girl had
died. Jesus said, "Do not be afraid, just believe" (Mark 5:36).
When they got to Jairus' house, everyone was sad. "The girl
is not dead. She is sleeping," Jesus said. Jesus sent everyone
away but the girl's parents. Then He took the girl by her
hand and said, "Little girl, I say to you, get up!" and the
girl was brought back to life (vv. 39–42)! This is only one of
the miracles Jesus did while He was on earth. Jesus is never
bothered when we pray and ask for His help. If there's something
you are praying for, don't lose hope. Keep praying.
Jesus hears you.

• •

Jesus, even when it seems that You won't
give me what I'm praying for, I will continue
to hope and trust in You. Amen.

Night 358
GOD'S EXCELLENT PLAN

We are His work. He has made us to belong
to Christ Jesus so we can work for Him.
He planned that we should do this.

EPHESIANS 2:10

Jesus sets the example for how we should live. The more you learn about Him from the Bible, the more you can work at being patient, kind, loving, and caring, the way He is. You will learn to put what God wants before what *you* want, the way Jesus did. But what about His plan for your life? Pray and ask God about it. Read your Bible. God often speaks to us through His Word (Psalm 119:105). Then have faith that God will work out His plan for your life and that His plan is good. Trust God, and every day He will lead you toward His good plan—His *excellent* plan—for your life.

Father, what is Your plan for me? I know that it is good.
Speak to me through prayer and Your Word. Amen.

Night 359
BE GOOD, DO GOOD

But God, the One Who saves, showed how
kind He was and how He loved us.

TITUS 3:4

✳

In Paul's letter to Titus, he wrote about how people who
love Jesus should behave. They should respect authority,
not say bad things about anyone, live in peace, and have a
humble attitude.

Paul also reminded his friends to remember their behavior before they met Jesus. It was only when Jesus came into
their hearts that those behaviors changed. Paul knew what
he was writing about. He once hated others and approved
of the mistreatment of those who believed in Jesus. Paul
wasn't about peace at all. But then Jesus came (Acts 9:1–19).
Suddenly Paul exchanged his bad behavior for the kind of
behavior that showed Jesus was inside his heart.

Jesus, I'm so thankful that You came
into my heart. You make me want to
be good and do good things. Amen.

Night 360
KEEP THE LIGHT BURNING

*"While I am in the world,
I am the Light of the world."*

JOHN 9:5

*

The Old Testament is about life before Jesus. It contains stories about people misbehaving and displeasing God. But throughout the Old Testament, we see that God continued to love us. The New Testament is all about Jesus! When He came, it was like God's love began to shine a bright light on the world. As Jesus spread God's message to the people, God's light grew brighter. Then Jesus did the greatest thing of all—He died on the cross so our sins would be forgiven and we would go to heaven someday! Jesus said that while He was in the world, He was the light. Now it's our turn to keep His light burning. We do that by telling others about Him and His way to heaven.

Jesus, I will keep Your light burning brightly.
I will tell all my friends about You. Amen.

Night 361
HOW TO BEST LIVE FOR GOD

This is the reason we do not give up. Our human
body is wearing out. But our spirits are getting
stronger every day. The little troubles we suffer
now for a short time are making us ready for the
great things God is going to give us forever.

2 CORINTHIANS 4:16–17

When you look at old people, what do you see? Their skin
has wrinkles. Their hair might be gray. Some walk slowly
and have trouble getting around. But what you see on the
outside isn't what's on the inside. Paul said that the human
body wears out but the spirit inside grows stronger. That
strength comes from many years of wisdom and especially
from living for Jesus. Christians grow old looking forward
to life in heaven. Many old people continue to serve God
through their communities and churches. And old people
are great at giving advice because they've gathered lots of
wisdom. Learn from them how to best live for God.

Father, lead me to older adults who
can teach me more about You. Amen.

Night 362
MORNING STAR

"I am Jesus. . . . I am the bright Morning Star."
REVELATION 22:16

***

The sun is the closest star to earth, and without it we couldn't exist. Everything about the sun works perfectly to sustain life on earth because God planned it that way. In addition to providing for life, God made the sun to give us beautiful sunrises and sunsets. Most mornings, the eastern sky is ablaze in colors of orange, red, pink, and yellow—a warm-up act for that moment when the brilliant morning star peeks over the horizon. It's no wonder that Jesus compared Himself to the sunrise. He is the Light of the World! His love shines bright like the morning star. So whenever you see a sunrise or feel the warmth of the sun on your skin, think of Him!

Jesus, Your love shines like the sun.
It warms me and gives me everything I
need to live. Thank You, Jesus. Amen.

Night 363
BE READY

On the day He comes, His shining-greatness will be seen in those who belong to Him. On that day, He will receive honor from all those who put their trust in Him.

2 THESSALONIANS 1:10

✦

Throughout his life, Paul had plenty of trouble. . .mostly because he wasn't shy about sharing the good news. Still, Paul never lost faith in Jesus. He trusted in the Lord and talked often about getting to heaven. But it wasn't enough for Paul to be content that he had a place there. He wanted the whole world to believe and be saved! This is the hope all Christians have—that everyone will believe and be saved. The Bible tells us that one day Jesus is coming back to earth. And everyone will see Him, and all who love and trust Him will honor Him. Those who have not accepted Him as Savior will be punished and sent away forever. Be ready. Honor Him every day.

I look forward to meeting You face-to-face, Jesus, whether here on earth or in heaven. Amen.

Night 364
THE DAY JESUS COMES

Make the best use of your time.
These are sinful days.
EPHESIANS 5:16

※

Maybe Jesus will come back to earth in your lifetime, or maybe not. The Bible tells us that no one but God knows the date or the time of day when He will return (Matthew 24:36). And because we don't know, we need to be ready. Every day, as you've read this book, you learned something new. You have a long life ahead, so take everything you learn and use it to serve God and others. Do your best to follow God's commands. Share the good news so more people will accept Jesus as their Savior. Make the best use of your time by making good choices and loving the Lord with all your heart. If you do these things, then you will be ready for Jesus!

* * *

Help me to use my time wisely. Make me
ready for the day You come, Lord. Amen.

Night 365
COMING SOON

Amen.

REVELATION 22:21 NIV

✳

One simple word, *Amen*. It means "let it be so." You've learned that God gave us every word of the Bible. He makes it come alive as we read. The Bible is like a textbook for Christians. It teaches God's rules and how He wants us to live. There are thousands of God's promises to us in the Bible, including the most important one—His promise of forever life through Jesus. Everything in the Bible is 100 percent true. God warns that no one should ever add to His words or take away any part that tells what will happen in the future (Revelation 22:18–19). And, just before the Bible ends, God reminds us of one big promise: Jesus is coming soon (v. 20). Let it be so. Amen!

• •

God, thank You for the Bible and all that You've taught me so far. Remind me to keep reading Your Word. I want to learn more. Amen.

SCRIPTURE INDEX

OLD TESTAMENT

CHECK OUT THESE FUN FAITH MAPS!

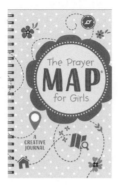

The Prayer Map for Girls
978-1-68322-559-1

The Prayer Map or Boys
978-1-68322-558-4

These prayer journals are a fun and creative way to fully experience the power of prayer. Each page guides you to write out thoughts, ideas, and lists. . .creating a specific "map" for you to follow as you talk to God. Each map includes a spot to record the date, so you can look back on your prayers and see how God has worked in your life.

Spiral Bound